9/14

Cultural Heritage
of Turkey

by

Zeynep AHUNBAY

REPUBLIC OF TURKEY
MINISTRY OF CULTURE AND TOURISM PUBLICATIONS

© **Republic of Turkey Ministry of Culture and Tourism**
General Directorate of Libraries and Publications
3230

Handbook Series
9

ISBN: 978-975-17-3448-8

www.kulturturizm.gov.tr
e-mail: yayimlar@kulturturizm.gov.tr

Photographs: Grafiker Ltd. Şti. Archive, Zeynep Ahunbay,
Umut Almaç, Mine Esmer, Nimet Hacikura,
Sinan Omacan, Robert Ousterhout, Levent Özgün,
Nazlı Özgün, Işıl Polat, Mustafa Sayar, Aras Neftçi

Third Edition
Kalkan Printing and Binding co. Print run: 5000.
Printed in Ankara in 2013.

Zeynep Ahunbay is professor at Istanbul Technical University, Faculty of Architecture, Department of Restoration

Ahunbay, Zeynep
   Cultural Heritage of Turkey / Ankara: Ministry of Culture and Tourism, 2013.
   198 p.: col. ill.; 20 cm.- (Ministry of Culture and Tourism Publications; 3230. Handbook Series of General Directorate of Libraries and Publications: 9)
   ISBN: 978-975-17-3448-8
   I. title. II. Series.
791.53

TABLE OF CONTENTS

Note on Usage

Modern Turkish uses the Latin alphabet, modified to ensure that there is a separate letter for each main sound. The spelling thus aims at phonetic consistency. For Turkish artists, place names, publications and special terms this book employs modern Turkish spelling. Proper names have been kept in modern Turkish with one exception – İstanbul has been rendered with normal English spelling using I rather than İ unless it is part of a title. Consonants have more or less the same sound as in English, except for:

c like j in English

ç like ch in English

ğ the "soft g". Depending on the adjoining letters, this is dropped, pronounced like y in English, or treated as lengthening the preceding vowel.

ı is a back, close, unrounded vowel which does not exist in English, the nearest equivalent being the phantom vowel in the second syllable of rhythm.

ö like ö in German or eu in French peur

ş like sh in English

ü like ü in German or u in French

PREFACE

Cultural heritage of a country reflects its life style and the creative power of its people. Living cultures foster their heritage; an encounter with them gives one the chance to have direct experience and appreciation. But access to the vanished civilizations is only possible through historical research and careful study of the physical. The unique artistic and scientific accomplishments of bygone cultures are regarded as part of the collective heritage of mankind; they contribute to the building up of a united picture of the world's cultural history.

Anatolia has been the scene of great cultures; archaeological researches in Turkey revealed spectacular sites from Neolithic, Hittite, Phrygian, Urartian, Hellenistic, Roman, Byzantine and Seljuk cultures. The knowledge gained from these finds is shared by scholars, but it is important to disseminate this information to wider circles, in order to make more people aware of the rich human experience reflected by these sites.

This book on Cultural Heritage of Turkey tries to bring together Turkey's World Heritage sites and the properties on the preliminary list. The initiative of the Turkish Ministry of Culture and Tourism to focus on publications is a chance to make these cultural assets known to the world. It also offers an opportunity to increase the awareness of the problems and to inspire new ideas for research and artistic creation.

Turkey's cultural heritage embodies a rich repertoire of monuments and sites from different periods and traditions. At the moment there are ten sites: Troy, Hattusha, Nemrut Dağ, Xanthos and Letoon, Hierapolis, Cappadocia, Istanbul, Great Mosque and Hospital in Divriği, Safranbolu and Selimiye Mosque and its Social Complex on the World Heritage List. Most of these sites are archaeological, representing the cultural diversity from about 2000 BC to the medieval period.

The tentative list reflects the variety and richness of the cultural heritage in Turkey. Karain, and Çatalhöyük, sites with the earliest marks of human existence in Turkey are included. There are also several very representative and well preserved archaeological sites from Hellenistic, Roman and Byzantine periods. Ephesus is one of them. Some historic cities with medieval foundations, like Mardin and Alanya, are also included. An outstanding Ottoman monument, Selimiye, the masterpiece of the renowned Mimar Sinan is also included.

The concept of "common heritage", coined by UNESCO, brings in new dimensions to cultural heritage protection. Common heritage means common responsibility. UNESCO and the member states to the World Heritage Convention try to overcome the difficulties of conservation in the world by offering technical and budgetary support to state parties which are in need. One of the important missions of the World Heritage Center is to offer help to improve the protection of cultural heritage worldwide.

Protection of universal values against emerging global threats is a challenging issue for the international society. It is a time of cultural awakening and taking action for all cultures of the world, which are fragile and threatened by neglect or pressure of migration, mass tourism, new development, engineering projects, mining, extensive renovations. The management problems have to be overcome. To protect urban identities, it is essential to revive traditional arts and skills. It is important to promote the protection of our common cultural and natural heritage. For the enhancement of protection activities, this book, a concise source about the World Heritage sites in Turkey, may serve as a communication tool. There is no doubt that knowing more will lead to better appreciation and care for protection. It is great pleasure to collaborate for the preservation of cultural heritage. Let's work together and celebrate the well being of our common heritage!

Zeynep Ahunbay, Istanbul 2011

I. PREHISTORIC SETTLEMENTS AND ANCIENT SITES

Caves were inhabited for long periods of time in the history of mankind; for the hunter gatherers, caves located near rivers or lakes were ideal because they afforded a chance for fishing and hunting. Among these, the Yarımburgaz cave near Küçükçekmece Lake is famous with its vestiges from the Lower Paleolithic period. According to anthropologists, man's ancestors originated about 1500000 years ago in east Africa and migrated to other parts of the world. Yarımburgaz cave, which consists of two chambers, is considered to be a stopping point for men travelling from Africa towards Europe. Inhabited by humans from the Middle Pleistocene period, this cave is an important site taking us back 300000 years in history.

KARAİN

Karain is considered to be the site with the earliest signs of human habitation in Anatolia. It is situated in the southern part of Turkey, about thirty kilometers to the northwest of Antalya. The location is within the Taurus mountain range, quite close to the strait of Çubuk, which permitted access from the Mediterranean coastal area to the central part of Anatolia.

Karain, meaning "the Dark Cave" is near Yağca Köy, on the slope of Çadır Tepe, which is 150 m above the travertine plain. According to geologists, the flat area at the foot of the hill had a lake in Pleistocene era. The fertile plain, the lake and water springs must have made the location attractive to the early settlers.

Karain is one of the large natural caves in Turkey. It consists of three chambers separated from each other by calcite walls and narrow passageways. Presence of stalactites and stalagmites make the interior spectacular. The total depth is about 50 meters. On the exterior of the cave, there are inscriptions in Greek. Several niches were carved on the rock surface at a later period.

The first excavations in the cave were conducted by I. Kılıç Kökten from Ankara University in 1946; researches continued until 1961. Eight layers from the end of Lower Paleolithic (250000-100000 BC) to the Roman period were uncovered. Archaeological researches continue in and around Karain under the leadership of Prof. I. Yalçınkaya from Ankara University, who collaborates with experts from other universities among which there is the University of Liege.

The site is unique, providing undisturbed layers from the Paleolithic era to the Roman period. It is also significant as the site which provided remains of homo neanderthalensis, the Neanderthal man. Fossils of extant mammals provided information about the fauna and climate conditions during the Pleistocene era. Paleolithic period is considered to be the first page of civilization. Paleolithic man gathered his food by hunting. Hand axes and scrapers were the first tools. Traces of animals like bison, ox, horse, deer, cow, bear suggest that the inhabitants were good hunters. Tools made from bones, hand axes and flint stones were among the finds from the cave. A stove and some firewood from the Middle Paleolithic period is regarded as an indication that the inhabitants had discovered fire and developed utensils for cooking. Religious beliefs appeared during the last period of the Paleolithic era; in Karain, the walls of the cave were adorned by pictures of the animals like goats and deer.

GÖBEKLİTEPE

Located near Urfa in southeast Turkey, Göbeklitepe is an archaeological site incorporating impressive remains from the early Neolithic period. Archaeologists think that the finds which go back to 9500 BC, belong to cult buildings and the neighboring settlement from the beginning of settled life. Excavations which started in 1995 by the German Archaeological Institute continue, revealing vestiges which relate to the history of the place. Colossal piers with snake, bird, bull, ram, leopard and spider figures have been exposed. Natural bedrock was shaped to serve as the floor;

walls arranged in a ring form surrounded the living spaces. Geophysical investigations showed that the site has more of the round buildings. Situated in a rural landscape, Göbeklitepe is an extraordinary place connecting modern man to his roots in the ancient world. The quality of the carvings and the size of the re-used stone piers make the site unique.

ÇATALHÖYÜK

Çatalhöyük is a Neolithic site located near Çumra, 52 km to the southeast of Konya. As one of the earliest known settlements on earth, the site has a high scientific value. The word Çatalhöyük means *the forked mound;* there are two tumuli very close to each other. The one on the east belongs to the Neolithic, the western one is from the Calcholithic era. The eastern tumulus is about 21 meters high and covers an area of roughly 500 by 300 meters. The site was discovered by the English archaeologist James Mellaart. The excavations he conducted between 1961-1965 gave exciting results, making the site internationally known. A total of 103 houses and 63 temples were unearthed. The striking feature of the houses was that they were built next to each other and did not have windows on their walls. Instead of streets, some courtyard like open spaces were left in between the houses. Access to the houses were through small openings at the top of the walls. People entered the houses by using ladders; the ladders were drawn in at night. It is estimated that the site was inhabited by 8000 people.

The dwellings consist of a large hall and small adjacent rooms. In the main rooms, there are raised platforms for sitting and lying down. One or more hearths, a furnace attached to the southern wall were the basic furniture of the dwellings. The smaller rooms, which were probably used for storage, were accessed by narrow passages. The walls are made of adobe, with timber posts placed inside them for structural reinforcement. The floors and wall surfaces were plastered with white clay. The upper structures were made of timber beams. The roofs were flat and covered with earth.

The plans of the buildings were very similar; they were named as house or temple according to their inner arrangement and furniture. In the temples there were small and large bull heads, horns, paintings and reliefs. These finds provided information about the life and burial traditions of the inhabitants. Many figurines were found during the excavations. Mother goddess cult and burial traditions are interesting. The Neolithic society of Çatalhöyük considered nature as a woman and the fertility of nature was depicted as plump woman goddesses. In female figures, the limbs and breast are overemphasized. The dead were buried in the main rooms, under the floors.

Red, yellow, black and green paint on white plaster background was used in the wall paintings. The artworks were dedicated to the ancestors. In addition to goddess and human figures, there are also depictions of animals like the leopard, deer, bull and vulture on the walls. There are panels with hunting, dancing and burial scenes. A landscape panel with a volcano in the background was interpreted as the eruption of Hasan Dağ by J. Mellaart. Some of the interesting finds from the the 1960's excavation were moved to the Museum of Ancient civilizations in Ankara and are exhibited there.

Çatalhöyük, Shelter designed by Architect S.Omacan
(photo courtesy of S. Omacan)

Since 1993 Ian Hodder from Stanford University is leading the excavations in collaboration with an international team of archaeologists. He started a 25 year program which aimed at research using the latest technology. The site is difficult to preserve due to its deeply stratified deposits represented by phases of mudbrick structures. Painted wall decorations are fragile and their long term survival in the open is impossible. The team was determined to stop erosion. Conservation laboratories were established at the site to consolidate and preserve some of the weak and sensitive elements. After conservation treatment, some of the finds were transferred to the Museum of Konya and are exhibited there.

Recent research revealed more details about the life at the settlement. It was discovered that people lived there since 7400 BC. Their economy depended largely on agriculture and animal husbandry. Their fields were about 10 km away from the mound. The sheep and goats were domesticated but cattle was wild and lived in the nearby swamp. The second tumulus is dated to the Chalcolithic era, dating from 6000- 5500 BC. Recent researches have shown that the western mound was inhabited after the Neolithic tumulus was deserted.

One of the important activities of the research team was to develop a management plan for the site. A lot of effort was put to increase the interest at the site and make Çatalhöyük a tourist destination. Interpretation was developed through a small visitor center established in a reconstructed Çatalhöyük house. Guided tours and a reconstructed experimental house help the visitors to understand the site better. A 27x 45 m protective roof was designed for the southern part of the site and thus an area with 20 houses was opened to visitors in 2003. A second shelter with a span of 28 meters was designed and executed by Architect Sinan Omacan in 2008

The Near East was the cradle of Neolithic culture which brought about the transition from hunter-gatherer to settled society with a life based on agricultural activity. Çatalhöyük is unique as a pioneering Neolithic site with its large size and dense occupation, as well as its artistic production: spectacular wall paintings, exotic bulls and mother goddesses.

EPHESUS

Ephesus is about 60 km to the south of Izmir; next to the small town of Selçuk. In Antiquity, it was one of the important port cities of the Aegean, from which roads commenced towards the eastern provinces. Being situated close to the mouth of the river Caystrus, the harbour had serious problems of silting. After almost two thousand years, Ephesus has become an inland site with only archaeological remains indicating its relation to the sea.

The ancient site of Ephesus covers a very wide area, with remains from Hellenistic, Roman and Byzantine periods. Excavations which started in the nineteenth century go on revealing more and more of the significant elements of the city. The earliest vestiges of settlement around Ephesus are from the Late Chalcolithic, about 5000 BC. According to legend, Greek colonists lead by Androclus came to the site around the 10th century BC and settled near a shallow inlet of the sea, which at the time extented as far as where the stadium stands today. The area was already inhabited by Carians and Lelegians.

The origin of the name Ephesus is probably the Hellenized form of Apasa. The largest temple of the cult of Artemis was located in Ephesus. The archaic temple burned in 356 BC and was reconstructed in the fourth century BC. Several famous artists contributed to the rebuilding with their works, thus the Temple of Artemis Ephesia was became of the seven wonders of the ancient world.

The region went under Lydian and Persian rules; several changes took place following natural disasters, occupations and political decisions. After destroying the earlier city, Lydian king Croesus established a settlement near the Artemision. By 287 BC, this city had become stagnant due to the silting of its harbour. King Lysimachus wanted to move the city from the flat area towards the south, to the area between the hills of Bülbüldağ (Mount Koressos) and Panayır

Dağ (Mount Pion). His city, named *Arsinoeia* was laid out with a grid plan and provided the facilities of a Hellenistic city. He erected a 9 km long wall to surround the city, part of which still stands. The agora and the theater were two of the important elements of this planning. The commercial market, named *Tetragonos Agora* was located in the flat area to the west of the so called *Marble Street*. The square form of the commercial agora as it is seen today was the result of a complete rebuilding on a larger area in the late 1st century BC. Prytaneion was the second important structure of the city after the Temple of Artemis. It was the city hall where official guests were entertained and banquets took place. The holy fire of Hestia burned in it continuously.

Roman Emperor Antoninus Pius raised Ephesus to the status of the capital of the Province of Asia, the city where the Roman proconsul resided. On the flat area between the Panayırdağ and Bülbüldağ, the administrative center of the city developed during the time of the Emperor Augustus.

The city became very prosperous and it flourished, reaching its peak in the second century AD. It was embellished with

Ephesus, Temple of Hadrian

beautiful monuments. Ephesus was estimated as the fourth largest city in the east of Rome after Alexandria, Antioch and Athens. The harbour was connected to the theater by a 528m long road, which took its final form during the reign of Emperor Arcadius (395- 408 AD). The colonnade, known as Arcadiane, was 11 meters wide and in the fifth century it was equipped with street lighting.

The main street connecting Bülbüldağ and Panayırdağ was paved with marble and lined with colonnades. Public buildings like the Nympaeum of Trajan, Varius Bath and Temple of Hadrian were erected on the north side of the lower part and tombs and honorific monuments on its south side. The richly furnished private houses of the city developed on the slopes above the administrative district. Several earthquakes damaged the monuments and the city, during its long history. The temple of Artemis was destroyed by an earthquake in 262. There were other strong earthquakes in the 3rd quarter of the 4th century.

Ephesus became a Christian city from 350 AD. Several buildings in the city were converted into churches. The spiritual and physical center during the early Christian period was the Church of Mary, consecrated to the mother of God. One of the most impressive monuments near the harbour, the so called Serapeion, was also converted into a church. In the sixth century, a four column monument with the statues of the evangelists standing at their top, was erected in the middle of the Arcadiane.

It is believed that St. John was buried at Ayasuluk/Hagios Theologos around the beginning of the second century. A church was built in his memory in the fourth century, which was remodelled on a grander scale during the Justinian period.

By 654 the first Arab attacks started. A new wall surrounding the Coressian quarter was built to protect the city from the incursions. The Hellenistic and early Roman center was left out of the new Byzantine fortification. Thereafter the seat of the bishop was moved to the Church of St. John at the Ayasuluk Hill. Seljuk Turks arrived in the region in the fourteenth century. They settled to the northeast, close to the citadel of St. John, where İsa Bey Mosque and other monuments from the Principality of Aydınoğulları are located.

The first digs in Ephesus were conducted on behalf of the British Museum by J.T. Wood, architect and engineer. He located the Temple of Artemis and excavated there in 1871. In 1895, Professor Otto Benndorf from the Department of Classical Archaeology at the University of Vienna, obtained a permit and started the excavations. Except the two world wars (1914-1925 and 1936-1954), the Austrian Archaeological Institute has been working at Ephesus. The agoras, the main theater, baths, temples, terrace houses and many other buildings have been excavated and presented to the public.

Over the years, many of the excavated monuments were evaluated for possibilities of anastylosis. There are several examples of good quality research and execution. It is possible

Ephesus, Library of Celsus

to follow the change in attitude towards the restoration of the archaeological finds. Starting with middle of the twentieth century, fountains, tombs, houses and the theater have been studied and restored. One of them is the Nymphaeum of Trajan, which had a two storey tabernacle façade. It was built in honour of Emperor Trajan who visited Ephesus in 113-114. An architectural installation was carried out in 1962. The columns were missing so the restoration cautiously did not attempt to reconstruct them. The architectural elements were arranged, according to their original position in the monument. The reconstruction drawing gives an idea about the original look of the monument.

Temple of Hadrian is a small temple like monument which was incorporated into the Varius Bath complex on Curetes Street, "in homage to Emperor Hadrian". The anastylosis of the portico, which was carried out in late 1950's by architect F. Göschel is successful, giving the full scale of the monument, without going into the reconstruction of lost elements.

A.Bammer worked on the Temple of Artemis, Memmius Monument, Pollio Monument, Fountain of Domitian and the Domitian's Terrace. In general, his works exhibit a personal approach, not respecting the rules of the Venice Charter. The re-erection of the Memmius Monument, one of the few examples of late Hellenistic monuments, is a modern interpretation, rather than a true anastylosis of the surviving elements.

One of the major achievements in Ephesus has been the anastylosis of the Celsus Library, which was founded in the name of the Roman senator Tiberius Julius Celsus Polemaeanus in 117. The monument was excavated in 1905/6; some of the architectural elements and statues were taken to Vienna and are in the Ephesus Museum now. But still a lot of the architectural blocks were preserved at the site. After a long research and documentation under direction of V.M. Strocka and architect F. Hueber, the Library façade was restored to its full height in the years 1970-78. It is one the focal points of the city and exhibiting the rich architectural details and beauty of the second century monument.

The north side of the Library Court is dominated by a monumental gate erected as a triumphal arch. It formed the south entrance from the enlarged Tetragonos Agora since Augustan times. The gate was re-erected between 1979-1988 under the direction of Architect F. Hueber. With the erection of the Gate, the Library Court became an enclosed space, giving the full scale of the place in the Roman era.

The excavations of the Terrace Houses at the foot of Bülbüldağ provided a lot of information about the urban life in Ephesus. Terrace House 1 is a housing block covering an area of 3000 square meters and has six residential units erected on three terraces. It was excavated between 1960-67 under the direction of H. Vetters. The oldest house in the block is from the first century BC. The second block of houses, which covers an area of 4000 square meters, was excavated between the years 1967-1983. The lowest terrace of the residential units opened on to the Curetes Street which runs between the Gate of Hercules and the Library of Celsus, contained workshops and taverns. The rich interior design of the atriums and the rooms with frescos and mosaics, marble panelling reflects the

Ephesus, Great Theater

high architectural quality of the villas. The site is protected by a shelter completed at the end of the twentieth century.

With its imposing theater, attractive monuments and terrace houses Ephesus is one of the most frequented archaeological sites of Turkey. It is unique in its rich collection of monuments with high quality of architectural design and decoration. It is a great task to keep the site in good condition against nature and the movement of large groups of visitors. The constant works by the local museum and the archaeological Institute help to maintain the site. The restoration of the theater is one of the projects which is on the agenda at the moment. Researches continue to learn more about the unexcavated areas; geophysical methods were used to find out about the earlier settlements, the location of streets and important remains.

APHRODISIAS

Aphrodisias is located in western Anatolia, within the province of Aydın. It lies on a plateau at the western foot of the 2308 m high Mt. Salbakus (Babadağ), near Karacasu. In antiquity, Aphrodisias was famous for her sculptors. With ample supply of marble from the nearby quarries, the sculptors of the Aphrodisian School produced works of art which can be seen in the ruins of the city and also in other parts of the Mediterranean.

With its interesting features, the site attracted the attention of travellers starting from the 17th century. The first excavation was lead by a Frenchman named P. Gaudin. It took place in 1904-5 at the Bath of Hadrian; the finds were transferred to the Archaeological Museum of Istanbul. In 1937, an Italian team directed by G. Jacopi started the excavation at the portico of Emperor Tiberius. There was a long intermission until researches were resumed in 1961 by Prof K. Erim from the University of New York. After thirty years of dedicated work, he succeeded in bringing to light the impressive monuments of the ancient town. During the excavations numerous inscriptions and sculpture were revealed. To present the finds to the public, a local museum was erected in 1979, within the square of the old Geyre village, to the east of the ancient city.

Aphrodisias has a special place in Turkish archaeology. There are many archaeological sites which are covered by traditional or modern settlements. In the case of Aphrodisias, the old village of Geyre had spread over the site. It was by the decision of the Ministry of Culture and the patient work of Professor Erim that the village was relocated and the land expropriated to the benefit of archaeology. By removing the village houses and expropriating the site, it was possible to continue the excavation and pave the way for the presentation of the site as an archaeological park.

The ancient city had not been walled until Late Roman period; a 3.5 km long circuit was constructed in 260, to protect her from the attacks of Goths. The city lies mostly on flat land, with only the 15-20 m high protuberance of the acropolis. The excavations at the acropolis have shown that it was a tumulus dating back to the Neolithic period.

The most revered monument of the city was the temple of Aphrodite. According to the evidence obtained from the researches, its construction started in the first century BC and was completed in the second century. The temple was a pseudodipteros in Ionic order. During the Byzantine period, it was converted into a church.

Another major monument is the theater, which could seat 10000 people. It is situated on the eastern slope of the acropolis hill. According to its inscription, it was founded by Julius Zoilos and completed in 27 AD. Most of the upper cavea is lost but the lower part was found in good condition. The theater was modified in the second century AD for gladiator plays and wrestling.

The city had several public spaces. The richly carved architecture of these buildings is one of the attractions of the city. The portico of Tiberius, which is next to the bath of Hadrian and Aprodite, is noteworthy with its elegant frieze decorated with masks and garlands. The Bath of Hadrian and Aphrodite is one of the most impressive buildings in the city. It was erected in honor of Emperor Hadrian's visit to the city. The agora is very spacious with its gigantic size, measuring 205 by 120 meters. The first century BC structure was enlarged in the second century. Second century was the brightest period of Aphrodisias. The Odeon of Aphrodisias, which could accommodate 1700 people is also from this time.

The stadium of Aphrodisias is located in the northern part of the city, next to the walls. The 262 m long and 59 m wide building seated 30000 people. Its sphendone was modified in the seventh century to adapt the building into an arena. It is the best preserved stadium in Asia Minor.

Conservation of the buildings and the artifacts was an important task for the archaeological team. Restoration of mosaic pavements and fresco fragments were carried out regularly by conservators. Many columns were re-erected. The site was surveyed and projects were developed for anastylosis. The restoration of the Tetrapylon leading to the temenos of the Temple of Aphrodite was one of such projects. With the technical support of Dr. F. Hueber from the Ephesus team, a project was developed. The original blocks belonging

Aphrodisias, Tetrapylon

to this important monument were reassembled between 1984 and 1990.

From 1979 onwards, a temple dedicated to Aphrodite, Emperor Augustus and the family of Emperor Julius Claudius was excavated. The temple was raised on a podium and was preceded by a marble street lined with three storey porticos on both sides. The façades of the porticos were enriched with beautiful reliefs. The whole complex was named Sebasteion by K. Erim, referring to the old Greek name of Emperor Augustus. A new museum was urgently needed to house the large number of exceptionally beautiful marble panels recovered during the excavation. The Ministry of Culture and Tourism supported the idea and the extension was realized.

Prof. K. Erim died in 1992. One of his last concerns was the protection of the ancient necropolis. Now, the excavations are directed by R.R.Smith. It is important to continue research and at the same time maintain the site which is unique with its setting and contents. The exceptional artistic quality and the natural beauty of the site deserves utmost care to sustain these qualities.

LYCIAN CITIES

Lycia is the ancient name of the southwest part of Turkey; the region stretched from Dalaman in the west to Phaselis near Antalya in the east. Its ancient borders were defined as the Aegean Sea in the west, Mediterranean in the south, Caria in the northwest, Phyrigia and Pisidia in the north and Pampylia in the east. Lycia is a rocky and mountainous region with a beautiful coast. The cedar forests on the Taurus mountains were famous for yielding tall and durable cedar trees which were used in ship building.

The name Lycia comes from Luku or Lugga people, who inhabited the region starting with 2000 BC. According to Herodotus, these people had migrated to mainland from Crete. Lycians were united in a League to act together in peace and war. Mountain barriers and the precipitious coastline helped them to defend their country. They resisted the Persian invasion but had to submit. The region was annexed to the Roman Empire in 43 AD.

The most important city of the Lycian League was Xanthos, with Letoon as the cult center (See Chapter V, Xanthos and Letoon). Myra, Tlos, Pınara, Patara and Olympos were the other five important cities of the region. Patara was the main harbour of Lycia. As the birthplace of Apollo, it was very important and a temple was raised in the god's name. Some of the other sites in the region are Limyra, Rhodiapolis, Telmessos, Arykanda, Sidyma, Pydnai, Antiphellos, Phellos, Apollonia, Teimiussa, Aperlai, Sura, Kibyra Maior, Oinoanda, Bubon and Balbura.

The most interesting monuments of the Lycians are their tombs), which are dated to the 6-5th century BC. In many places, the funerary architecture dominates the landscape. Tombs were cut into the rocks, creating spectacular combinations with other natural elements, like the sea or the trees. Two types of tomb were characteristic of the region. The first consists of a flat roofed burial chamber raised on a 3-6 meters high pier. These monuments resemble houses; they are decorated with reliefs depicting animals, hunting, cult and war scenes. Harpy tomb in Xanthos is a good example

22

Simena, sunken city

of the type. The second type is in the form of a sarcophagus, usually raised on a podium. The characteristic feature is the lid, which is shaped like a gothic arch.

KEKOVA

Kekova is a small island in the Mediterranean, located to the west of Antalya, between Kaş and Finike. The island and the neighboring mainland make up a very picturesque landscape. Several small ancient settlements, which were part of the Lycian League, existed along the coast and inland.

The Mediterranean coast is seismically active and Dolichiste, a Lycian settlement which existed between the coast and the island suffered from an earthquake; several urban and architectural elements like streets, quays, walls and stairs are in the water. To trace the remains of an ancient city under the water is an exceptional experience; it provides a chance to learn more about the natural history and the archaeology of the place.

Simena is the small ancient town across the Kekova island. It was united with Istlade, Aperlai Apollonia and Isında in the Lycian League. The ruins of a Roman bath stand near the shore. The inscription explains that it was dedicated to Emperor Titus (r. 79-81) by the people of Aperlai and the Lycian League. A small castle from the Byzantine period rises on the hillside; it has a small theater cut into the rock.

Aperlai is the town situated to the west of the Sıcak peninsula. Its history goes back to the 5th century BC. As a result of seismic action, its quay and harbour structures are under the waters of the bay. Another nearby small town is Teimioussa, which has a wonderful view over the Mediterranean. In the harbour, a tomb and some doors partially submerged in the sea are evidence of the seismic action. A small citadel is perched on the edge of a low cliff. Several house type tombs were cut into the rock.

PERGAMON

Pergamon is located in the western part of Turkey, near the modern town of Bergama. It was the capital of the Hellenistic kingdom of Pergamon which was founded in the 3rd century BC, after the death of Alexander the Great. Under king Eumenes, who lived in the second century BC, the city was adorned with impressive monuments. After the death of king Attalos III in 133, Pergamon became part of the Roman Empire; it continued to hold its importance during the Byzantine era.

The ancient city consists of the lower town and the acropolis perched on a high cliff, overlooking the plain. A cult center dedicated to Asclepius was developed within the lower part of the town. Today the remains of the ancient town, consisting of palaces, temples, agoras, theaters make the site one of the major attractions of the ancient world. The site is located in an earthquake prone region and major monuments have been subjected to seismic activity over a long period of time. The temples, high retaining walls collapsed and were covered with earth. Excavations at the site started in 1878 by German archaeologists, Carl Humann, A. Conze and R. Bohn. The Altar of Zeus was one of the important discoveries. This great work of art from the Hellenistic period was transferred to Berlin and is now exhibited there. Excavations continued in the 20 th century by the German Archaeological Institute; much of the city and many of the monuments were revealed, restored and presented to the public. Especially the anastylosis of the stoa and the temple of Trajan during the second half of the 20 th century are noteworthy. Some of the mosaics and important decorative elements were protected in situ under new shelters. Recently, work has been going on in the lower city to preserve and present the site to the inhabitants and the visitors.

Pergamon, Temple of Trajan restored by the German
Archaeological Institute (DAI) (1974-1994)

PERGE

Perge, one of the important cities of Pamphylia, "the land of
all tribes", is located 18 km to the east of Antalya. As one
aproaches the site from the small town of Aksu, the first
thing that catches the eye is the most prominent structure of
the ancient city, the theater. The stadium, Late Roman and
Hellenistic gates support the impression of the image of a
grand city.

Perge was visited by several travellers in the nineteenth
century and documented. But real archaelogy started in the
twentieth century by Professor A.M. Mansel from Istanbul
University. He and his successor Prof. J. Inan revealed most
of the city; the Hellenistic entrance with towers, the oval
courtyard behind it, the arch of Hadrian, the agora, the
colonnaded streets, the Demetrios Apollonios Arch and many
others. Excavations brought to light many interesting small
finds, but the most exciting were the magnificient statues
which are now exhibited in the Museum of Antalya.

Prof. H. Abbasoğlu has been leading the excavations since
1988. Recent research and excavations under his direction
revealed finds going back to early Bronze Age (4th-3rd millenia
BC). He also devoted attention to studies on the urban
fabric and funerary architecture of the site. The necropoli
were investigated, uncovering interesting wall paintings and
funerary objects.

During the long years of dedicated to the site, several anastylosis projects were realized in the agora and the collonnaded streets. The dangerous walls in the south bath were consolidated. A restoration project was developed for the triumphal arch of Demetrios Apollonius. Conservation of mosaics, wall paintings were carried out regularly. At the moment the critical state of the Hellenistic towers is in focus; measures to keep them standing are being investigated.

Perge is a grand site with impressive remains. The fact that it has been preserved with almost all of its elements, is very important. Excavations provided a lot of new information which make it possible to follow the growth of the city from ancient times to the Hellenistic period and through the Roman era. Careful researches and conservation work are needed to sustain the integrity and beauty of the site.

SAGALASSOS

Sagalassos is a spectacular site on top of Mt. Akdağ, which overlooks the nearby valley of Ağlasun. This are was called Pisidia in ancient times; it is the hinterland of Pamphylia and river Caystros flowing down from here reaches Perge and the Mediterranean. Due to the difficulties of reaching it, the site was untouched until late 1980's. Professor Marc Waelkens from Belgium has been working at Sagalassos since 1990's. After years of careful multidisciplinary work, major elements of the city were brought to light, conserved and presented to the public.

According to recent research, settlement in the region goes back to prehistoric era, but most of the fabric of the present Sagalassos dates from Hellenistic to Byzantine periods. The city was protected by walls in the Hellenistic period. As it grew in the Roman period, the fortifications had to be expanded to protect the newly developed areas. The important buildings of the city were organized around several terraces on the hillside. The main road running connected the agoras at two different levels. The lower agora had the Roman baths and several other buildings around it. The

Sagalassos, detail from the Heroon frieze

upper agora was surrounded by the city hall, Doric Temple, a fountain, the Library of Neon, workshops and the theater. Earthquakes in the sixth century destroyed the city and lead to its abandonment. Researches conducted in the last twenty years have contributed a lot to the understanding of the site and its protection. After a survey of the surrounding area, action was taken to protect the beautiful landscape by urban planning measures. Restoration of the Doric fountain revived the functionality of the Late Hellenistic monument which had its fresh water supply from the mountain. The beautiful mosaic floor of the Nero Library was protected by a shelter. Heroon is another significant monument which has been restored. It is a 14 meter high tomb, with a magnificient frieze of dancers in high relief at its base. The restoration of the Antonine Nymphaeum attached to the north wall of the Upper Agora is another project which has contributed to the attraction of the site.

TERMESSOS

Termessos is located to the north of Antalya, on Güllük Dağ which is on the Taurus range. This part of Anatolia was the borderland between Pamphylia and Pisidia in ancient times. The remains of the ancient town are high up on a hill, which rises 1050 above the sea. The city is a Hellenistic settlement which was developed by the Romans. Due to the steep hills, the city was not surrounded by a continuous circuit of walls. The site is spectacular with its impressive monuments and vistas from the top of the hill down into the Mecine Canyon. The ruins are surrounded by a thickly wooded forest. Due to its rich flora and fauna, the area is protected as a National Park.

Some researchers visited the site in the nineteenth century and made surveys of the surviving structures. Parts of the city walls, towers, the King's Road, Hadrian's gate, gymnasium, agora, theatre, an odeon, richly decorated tombs, cisterns and a drainage system are still standing in good condition. No excavation has been conducted yet at this thicky wooded site. Prof. V. Çelgin has conducted extensive research on inscriptions, especially those in the necropoli.

Termessos, theater

II. MEDIEVAL SITES

Medieval period of Anatolia is represented by monuments and sites from Byzantine and Seljuk cultures. Constantinople and Cappadocia were important centers for Byzantine art and architecture in the middle ages (see Chapter V, Göreme National Park and Rock Sites of Cappadocia and Historic Areas of Istanbul). Cities and monuments which were significant centers for Seljuk culture and Islamic architecture will be presented in chapters III and IV.

MYRA AND ST. NICHOLAS CHURCH

Myra comes from myrrh, the fragrant bitter gum tree which grows in the region. Myra, which is located to the west of Antalya, was one of the important cities of the Lycian League. A magnificient theater from the Roman era stands in Demre plain, next to the cliffs which are full of Lycian rock cut tombs. The combined image of the theater and the tombs on the high cliff is a unique composition, illustrating the achievement of man in shaping nature and integrating it with new works of art over the centuries.

Myra is an important place for Christians as well. St Nicholas, also known as Santa Claus was the archbishop of the area in the 4th century, was buried in Myra. The first church erected in his name collapsed as a result of an earthquake in 529. During Arab raids in the 7th and 9th centuries the city and the church were damaged. After being totally destroyed by Arabs in 1034, the church was reconstructed by Constantinos IX in 1043.

Travellers in the nineteenth century made observations about the church and the monastery nearby. In 1862, a project was initiated by Russians to restore the neglected church; A. Salzmann, a Frenchman worked on the church, reconstructing some of the missing elements of the upper structure. The belfry was added in 1876. Excavations around the church by Prof. Y. Ötüken in the twentieth century revealed interesting finds. The site is very popular; its relation with Santa Claus attracts visitors from all over the world.

TARSUS AND ST. PAUL'S WELL

Tarsus is an ancient Mediterranean city; during the Roman period it was surrounded by walls. Not much remains from the walls but there is the spectacular ruins of a Roman bath in the center. An excavation for a car park revealed the decumanus of the ancient city about 3 meters under the present ground level. The ancient street paving made of large basalt blocks has been preserved in very good condition. The remains of the colonnaded street and ruins from later periods in the center links present day Tarsus to its Roman past.

The relationship of Tarsus with St. Paul is well-known and considered important. Today there is no visible remains from him, but a church and some archaeological remains are related to him.

The historic center of Tarsus has a good repertoire of monuments from the medieval and Ottoman period. Especially the houses dating from the nineteenth century make up a nice traditional townscape. The Turkish Ministry of Culture and the Municipality of Tarsus have collabored on projects for the rehabilitation of the historic center.

ALAHAN MONASTERY

Alahan Monastery is located at the boundary of Central Anatolia and the Mediterranean region, between Karaman and Mut. The complex of Alahan consists of three churches, a baptistry, houses, caves, cells and tombs. The ruins cover roughly an area of 30x200 meters. The site was visited by several scholars in the nineteenth century; H. Laborde and A.C. Headlam published the first surveys and reports about the site. Prof. P. Verzone made a more detailed study of the site and published it in 1955.

Alahan Monastery provides a lot of information about the life of early Christian monastic life. An inscription found at the site dates the foundation of the complex to the first half of the fifth century. The stylistic connections with ancient architecture and the fine stone carving relates the building tradition to antiquity.

The first church which is located in the western end of the complex was the most important. Religious ceremonies were conducted there. Its eastern, southern and western walls are partially preserved. Second church, which was probably added later is also damaged. A portico extending along the whole length of the complex connected the three churches. Prof. P. Verzone named this arcade as *Via Sacra* and claimed that it was used for processions on holy days. People from outside could come here to visit the place.

The eastern church is the best preserved of the three. It measures 16x25 meters and is a three aisled basilica. It had a narthex with two floors. The transition to the dome which covered the central part of the basilica was by means of squinches. The remaining elements are excellent specimens illustrating the development of church architecture in early Christian period.

Alahan Monastery, general view from the portico towards the east

SÜMELA MONASTERY

Monastery of Sümela is located to the south of Maçka, on a 300 meters high steep cliff within Altındere valley. It was the largest convent of the region; it consists of six floors and has a total of 72 rooms. It had a library. The monastery is hard to reach; it can be accessed by climbing narrow steps on the hillside. The entrance is flanked by rooms for the guards. An aqueduct supplied fresh water to the monastery.

According to legend the monastery was founded by two priests from Athens around a natural cave that served as the church. Alexious Comnenos III supported the foundation of the complex in 1360. King Manuel II donated a piece of wood that is believed to be part of the cross on which Jesus Christ was crucified.

After Trabzon was annexed to the Ottoman Empire, Sultan Mehmet II granted the monastery the right to continue living at the same site. During the 18th century the duke of Wallachia made a donation for the restoration of the complex. The walls were decorated with frescoes; the complex was enlarged in 1749. Additional rooms for monks and guests were built in 1860. With the agreement for the exchange of people between Turkey and Grece, the monastery was deserted in 1923. At present, the Ministry of Culture and Tourism is responsible for the site. It is open to visitors.

Trabzon, Sümela Monastery

III. ANATOLIAN SELJUK ARCHITECTURE

AHLAT AND ITS MEDIEVAL CEMETERY

Ahlat is a small historic town on the western coast of Lake Van. It is located on a high plateau between Süphan and Nemrut Volcanos. The history of the place goes back to the Hurris in 4000 BC. From the eight century on, the region was dominated by Islamic states. Ahlat was one of the first places Turkish people settled in Anatolia. It has a long tradition of stone carving; the architect of Divriği Great Mosque and Hospital was from Ahlat (See Chapter V, Great Mosque and Hospital in Divriği).

The Turkish cemetery in Ahlat is famous with its collection of gravestones with exquisite workmanship. The graves have large stone slabs with rich decoration, mostly calligraphic, with verses from the Quran, hadiths or literary texts related to the dead person. Some are decorated with reliefs having geometric, floral or animal figures. The very large slabs are regarded as the transformed form of the pre-Islamic Turkish gravestone balbal under islamic influence.

There are also several tombs with square or polygonal plans and with pyramidal or conical caps. These buildings

Ahlat, grave stones

constitute of two parts. The underground burial chamber, the crypt, usually had the embalmed coffin of the deceased. The crypts were ventilated to keep the dead body in a good state of preservation. The upper chamber was like a small chapel for praying.

Ahlat has an extraordinary cultural landscape with its cemetery and funerary monuments, which reflect the high quality of stone carving of the medieval period. The stone of Ahlat comes from the Nemrut Volcano. It is light or dark brown, which gives a special tone to the grave stones and the monumental tombs. Ministry of Culture and Tourism is taking care of the site, trying to stop further deterioration and to improve the presentation.

DİYARBAKIR CITY WALLS

Diyarbakır, also known as Amid or Amida is an ancient city which is situated in southeast Turkey, within the Tigris valley. The city was a stronghold on the frontier between the Roman Empire and Persia. In 349 the walled city was enlarged and

Diyarbakır, folk dancing in front of the walls

some of the old parts were repaired by the Roman Emperor Constantius II. Between 367-375 the western walls were destroyed to enlarge the city. The walls and towers are full of inscriptions giving the dates of construction and later restorations.

Among the decorated towers, the Yedi Kardeş Tower is important with its inscriptions as well as double headed eagle and lion decoration. It was constructed in 1208 by the Artukid king Melik Salih. The architect was Yahya, son of Ibrahim.

Evli Beden was also constructed in 1208 under the Artukid king Melik Salih by the same architect. The inscription which surrounds the tower is a work of art.

Keçi Tower is located to the east of Mardin Kapı and is one of the oldest of the towers. It was restored in 1223 by Mervanids.

Tower of Nur, which is located next to Yedi Kardeş tower, was constructed by Seljuk sultan, Melik Shah in 1286. It is one of the most beautiful works of its period; decorated with symbols like horses, lions and deer figures.

The walls were surrounded by a lower circuit of front wall, but this has not come to our day; it was destroyed by the Ayyubid king Melik Kamil who took the city in 1232. The city has four gates: Tigris Gate/ New Gate in the east, Urfa Gate in the west, Dağ Kapı/ Harput Gate in the north and Mardin Gate in the south. The walls are 5 km long; there are 82 towers. The 12 meters high walls were built with local basalt stone. The thickness of the wall varies between 3 and 5 meters.

There is a citadel located to the northeast of the city. During the 16th century, under Süleyman the Magnificient, the citadel was enlarged. It has 4 gates and sixteen towers. Two of the gates open to the city and two to the outside.

Serious attempts have been made by the Municipality of Diyarbakır to clean the accretions to the walls. Ministry of

Culture has developed projects for the restoration of several wall sections and towers. At the moment a project is on the way to restore the buildings within the citadel and open them for cultural activities.

ALANYA CASTLE AND DOCKS

Alanya is a historic town on the southern coast of Turkey. It is situated on a small peninsula projecting towards the south, into the Mediterranean sea. The site was called Korakesion during the Hellenistic period. At the top of the promontory, there is an acropolis with the rest of a church and other medieval buildings.

Alanya became the harbour of the Anatolian Seljuk State under Sultan Alaeddin Keykubat. The name of the town changed to *Alaiye*, from which Alanya is derived. During the Seljuk period, the fortified city had a large keep near the harbour and the docks were erected right on the shore to build ships for the Seljuks. The 33 meters high octagonal tower built to protect the docks is called Kızılkule (Red Tower) and has several floors which now house the local museum. The survival of a medieval industrial plant which has been active until modern times is also very important feature for the coastal town.

The walls of the ancient castle are partially preserved, surrounding the old houses which date from late Ottoman

Alanya, general view from the east

period. The vernacular tradition is very important with its compatibility with the hot and humid climate. The houses are beautiful, with their verandas oriented towards the east. This arrangement creates a very impressive composition from the sea. Alanya has a nice combination of the hills and the sea. The caves. During the recent years the citadel has been researched and interesting historical information revealed from the medieval period.

ST. PETER'S CHURCH

Antioch is an important city in the eastern Mediterranean. It has an important place in the history of Christianity. Two of the Apostles, Saint Paul and Saint Peter met in Antioch. Saint Peter is regarded as the first bishop of the church founded in Antioch. Early Christians had to hide from the ruling Romans to come together and pray. It is believed that in Antioch, a natural cave at the foot of Mount Staurin was chosen as the secret meeting place of the Christians. The rock-cut church took its present form during the medieval era, when the city was occupied by the Crusaders in 1098. The church measures 9.5m wide, 13m deep and 7m high. The entrance façade was remodelled during a restoration in 1863. A small portion of the floor mosaic and wall paintings have survived. The historic and symbolic significance of the place is paramount.

Saint Peter's Church

Saint Peter's Church/ Antioch (Antakya)

KONYA, Capital of the Anatolian Seljuks

Seljuk Empire streched from Iran in the east, to central Anatolia in the west during the twelfth century. Under the Turkish rule, ancient Iconium became Konya and the center of administration for the Anatolian Seljuks.

The Anatolian Seljuks adorned their capital city with mosques, madrasas and civil buildings. Today, there is only the ruin of a tower from the palace of the Seljuk sultan. Yet the old mosque and several madrasas offer a good deal of information about the architecture of the medieval period. Stone, brick and glazed tiles were used to make a richly decorated architecture. Craftsmen from Iran and Syria came to the city to work on buildings, adorning them in the traditions of the architectural traditions they belonged to. İnce Minareli and Karatay madrasas are the most important from the thirteenth century. Alaaddin Mosque which was built above the ancient tumulus represents the multi columned mosque type common at this time. Tombs next to the mosque are significant with their designs and artistic details.

Konya is also well-known for Mevlânâ Celaleddin-i Rumi who was a great philosopher and writer. He founded the Mevlevi sect which opens its arms to all mankind. The tomb of Mevlana is a shrine which is visited by many people from all over the world. It is surrounded by a complex incorporating a convent and a public kitchen.

During the Ottoman period, the city was governed by crown princes. One of them was Selim II who was very attached to Konya and founded several monuments in the city and its vicinity. His mosque, which is attributed to Mimar Sinan is important for its position in the evolution of Ottoman mosque design.

Konya, tomb of Mevlana Celaleddin-i Rumi

SELJUK CARAVANSARAYS-
THE MEDIEVAL MONUMENTS
CONNECTED TO THE SILK ROAD

Caravansaray is a building type which has developed from
ribat, a military camp building located on the major roads
of Iran and Central Asia. When Seljuks came to Anatolia
and settled in the eastern part of the country, they needed
communication between cities. Travellers had to go over the
plains and mountain ranges for days, stopping at night in
places far away from inhabited areas. Robbers could attack
the caravans and take away the goods. This discouraged
travelling and made merchants hesitant to take risks. When
the flow of goods was not regular, the costs of merchandise
would rise and there would also be deficiency of some stuff
which was imported from far away countries.

To make travelling safe, caravansarays were built in the thirtienth century by the Anatolian Seljuks as an act of endowment. The travellers could stay three days free of charge. These foundations were established by the members of the imperial family and high officers of state. The travellers and their animals wer served meals as part of the service. This made it possible to activate trade on the route from China to Europe and also between the towns in Anatolia. As part of the medieval transportation and communication network, caravansarays are very significant buildings.

About 250 caravansarays have been spotted in Turkey. Of these eight were founded by the kings and are called sultan han. Most were built in the thirteenth century, when there was a lot of commercial activity and prosperity in Anatolia. Caravansarays are found on the road from the Black Sea to central Anatolia and down to the Mediterranean coast. From east to west, they were built at an interval of about 30 kilometers, the distance which a caravan could make in a day. During storms or bad weather the travellers would stay in the caravansaray and wait until the weather would permit them to move. The roof of the buildings are flat, which allowed the travellers to sleep on the roof during summer time.

The architecture of a caravansaray was suited to its purpose. The simplest form is a stable which accommodated both the animals and the travellers. A more developed form is the caravansaray with a courtyard and a closed section. The size of the courtyard and the program of spaces around it depended on the budget allocated for the building. In some there are rooms for storage, a bath, a kitchen a mascid and guard rooms. The size of the closed section varied according to the size of the donation. The simplest form is the caravansaray consisting of a courtyard surrounded by arcades. The earliest surviving example in Turkey is Evdir Han. The closed section can be a two, three or more aisled, vaulted building. Inside there are stone benches for the travellers. The animals would be tied to the piers; so the floor had to be cleaned every morning and drainage was very important.

The largest of the caravansarays are the sultan hans. The Sultan Han on the Konya Aksaray road is the largest in scale. It has been restored by the General Directorate of Pious Foundations. Sultan Han on the Kayseri-Sivas road is the second large of the type, covering 3900 square meters. It is rectangular in plan, with high walls and a portal in the middle of its entrance façade. The corners of the building are reinforced with cylindrical towers, adding strength to the robustness of the structure. Ağzıkarahan built in 1237 is very special among the extent caravansarays with its design, size and high level of workmanship. As sultan hans, it has a mescid in the center of the courtyard.

The so called enclosed type of caravansarays are very interesting with their stables arranged around a core with rooms encircling an inner courtyard. Mama Hatun Caravansaray in Tercan and Alarahan near Alanya are two examples of this typology. Most of the caravansarays were built of solid stone. They are monumental and impressive with their gigantic sizes and good quality stonework. From outside they look like castles, with high crenellated walls. In cases when there were attacks, they were to be defended as castles. The interiors are ventilated with slit windows and some openings at the top of the vaults.

IV. OTTOMAN MONUMENTS AND URBAN SITES

BURSA

Bursa has an exceptionally beautiful setting overlooking a fertile plane with Mount Olympos towering over the town. The hillside and the surrounding areas are full of trees and greenery, making the town known as *"green Bursa."* The Hellenistic settlement founded by the Bythinian King Prussia was surrounded by high walls. Under Ottomans the city developed outside of the walls; the complex of Orhan Bey was constructed in the 14th century; then Ulu Cami,

Bursa,entrance to Koza Han

the Great Mosque and several caravansarays were built making up a vast commercial center famous for its textiles, especially silk and velvet.

Hüdavendigar Complex at the heights of the Çekirge hills is one of the important mosques from early Ottoman architecture. Several early Ottoman imperial complexes founded by Yıldırım, Çelebi Mehmet and Murat II are located in this old capital and give the town its special character. The complex of Yeşil has a mosque, a madrasa, the tomb of the founder and a public kitchen. The mosque, the madrasa and the tomb are decorated with beautiful tiles from early fifteenth century. Craftsmen coming from the east worked in the design and decoration of these important monuments.

Bursa lost its position of being the capital city during late fourteenth century but it was still an important commercial center with its textile industry and silk trade. Bursa is also famous for its baths and spas. Natural hot water springs were used for curing several illnesses since the Romans. Ottomans built over the old baths or developed the tradition with many new spas and bathhouses, which are still favored for their curing capacities. The urban fabric of Bursa is very interesting with its colorful timber houses, some of which have survived in the walled city.

Prior to Ottoman siege and takeover of Bursa, several Turkish clans were settled around the city forming villages, which were called *kızıks*. Cumalıkızık is one of such villages; it is located on the northern foothill of Uludağ (the Olympos mountain) and surrounded by chestnut woods. The village has come to our day with its traditional life style and spatial organization. At the center there is the village square, surrounded by a mosque, a coffee house and some small shops. Timber houses with courtyards form the village.

EDİRNE and Selimiye Complex

Edirne is a historic city, the foundation of which goes back to Roman times. It was called Hadrianopolis, and the name was changed to Edirne after the city became the capital of the Ottomans in late fourteenth century. Until the conquest of Istanbul, it had the sultans palace and many fine monuments from the early Ottoman period are located in this beautiful town. Eski Cami, Üç Şerefeli, the bedesten and Mosque of Murat II, Bayezıt Complex from the end of the fifteenth century and several bridges are only some of the important monuments in this old capital.

46   Edirne, Selimiye, side elevation

Selimiye Mosque represents the climax of Architect Sinan's architectural career. The complex by Selim II was commissioned about 1570's. The program of the complex is not extensive as in the Süleymaniye in Istanbul; it consists of two madrasas, a primary school and a covered bazaar. The mosque was positioned at the highest point of the historic town and dominates the skyline. It is visible from far away and crowns the city.

The structural design and the interior space of the mosque are impressive. The eight piers that support the 30 m wide dome are elegant and the system permits for a less intrusive sizing of the structural members. There is no predecessor for this idea in early Ottoman architecture. It can be the Dome of the Rock in Jerusalem or the Sultaniye in Iran. The articulation of the buttresses on the exterior are very refined, as if carved by a sculptor. The incorporation of four minarets with the mosque creates a crystal like symmetry.

The mosque is mainly built with finely cut limestone; red stone and marbles are used to decorate the exterior. An arcaded courtyard with a low pool in the middle precedes the main space. The portico arcades are higher than the other sides, which emphasizes the entrance to the mosque. The interior consists of a space covered by a majestic dome suspended on eight piers. The mihrab is placed within a niche. The sultan's lodge, which is located at the northeast corner of the building, is adorned with fine stone carving and glazed tiles from Iznik.

Selimiye Mosque and its social complex were inscribed on the World Heritage List in 2011, on the basis of criteria (i) and (iv).

> i) The Selimiye Mosque Complex at Edirne is a masterpiece of the human creative genius of the architect Sinan, the most famous of all Ottoman architects in the 16th century. The single dome supported by eight pillars has a diameter of 31,5 m over a prayer space of 45X36m and with its four soaring minarets, it dominates the city skyline. The innovative

Edirne, Selimiye Mosque

structural design allowed numerous windows creating an extraordinary illuminated interior. The mosque complex was recognised by Sinan himself as his most important architectural work.

iv) The Selimiye Mosque with its cupola, spatial concept, architectural and technological ensemble and location crowning cityscape illustrates a significant stage in human history, the apogee of the Ottoman Empire. The interior decoration using Iznik tiles from the peak period of their production testifies to a great art form never to be excelled in this material. The mosque with its charitable dependencies represents the most harmonious expression ever achieved of the külliye, this most peculiar Ottoman type of complex.

MARDİN

Mardin is a historic city in southeast Turkey. It is perched on the southern slope of a hill overlooking the Mesopotamian plane. There is an acropolis at the very top of the hill with remains of some monuments.

The urban texture of Mardin consists of several medieval complexes and civil architecture arranged on terraces over the hillside. Several stone houses with beautiful arcades and carved façades make a beautiful composition. The narrow streets are surrounded by the walls which protect the courtyards from the gazes of strangers. Some streets have vaulted passages over them, connecting the spaces on two sides of the street. The street pattern is very complex and full of nice surprises.

The medieval city has several religious buildings, mosques, churches and madrasas, tombs. The commercial life is very active. Several inns and bazaars were built to accommodate travellers and craftsmen.

Mardin is famous with its multiethnic society. Besides muslims, there are Christians belonging to different sects. Monasteries were founded from early years of Christianity. Especially the Syriac church is well established in Mardin. Deyrulzaferan is a large complex situated about 10 kilometers from the east side of the town. The monastery started to develop around an earlier temple at the end of the fourth century. Some additions were made in the eighteenth century. The structure is well maintained by the Syriac society.

HARRAN AND URFA

Ancient Edessa is called Urfa today. Located in upper Mesopotamia, history of Urfa is connected to several prophets and their lives. Urfa is associated with prophets Hiob, Jethro and Abraham. According to legend, the pool next to the Great Mosque was created when prophet Abraham was put on the pyre. The firewood in the pyre became fishes. So, the pool and the fish in it are regarded as holy by the local people.

The architecture of Urfa is built with local limestone. Caravansarays and other traditional buildings, along with beautiful houses arranged around courtyards make up the historic urban core of this old city. There are attempts to preserve this important city and its rich cultural heritage.

Harran is an ancient site 44 km to the southeast of Urfa. It was the cult center of the Moon-god Sin. The name meant caravan route in Akkadean language. It was on the caravan route connecting Mesopotamia to eastern Mediterranean. There are several cultural layers which have been investigated by Dr. N. Yardımcı. The prehistoric layer is found in the tumulus near the Great Mosque from early Islamic period. The impressive ruin of the Great Mosque with its 33 meters high minaret bears testimony to the outstanding architectural accomplishment from the eighth century. A university was associated with the mosque. Harran is also important for its rural housing which is peculiar with its conical roofs .

İSHAK PAŞA PALACE, DOĞUBAYEZIT

The late Ottoman palace of İshak Paşa is located in Ağrı province, near the Iranian border of Turkey. The complex is a castle like structure, overlooking a beautiful valley and Mount Ararat. The palace was constructed by a local governor family. Behlül Pasha, the father of İshak Pasha, started the project; it was completed in 1784, by his son Mahmut Pasha. The palace was the seat of government in the 18th century; it is organized around several courtyards. The first courtyard was reached by a monumental portal with muqarnas decoration. There are several guard rooms and services around the first courtyard. In the second courtyard, there is a mosque and the tomb of the founder and his wife.

The third part was the harem, with a big kitchen, a dining room and apartments for the family.

The complex is very interesting with its general siting and details. There is no similar country house or palace from the Ottoman period in the provinces. The revival of Seljuk architecture in the tomb, the portals and the rich use of stone decoration makes the complex unique for its time and the region.

Doğubayezıt, Ishak Paşa Palace

V. WORLD HERITAGE SITES OF TURKEY

Turkey is a country very rich in cultural heritage. The early forms of human life on earth has its vestiges in the form of cave dwellings, mounds and prehistoric settlement. As an area located in the ancient world, many places are related to the ancient civilizations, Egyptian, Persian, Hellenistic and Roman cultures had their influence in the lands which make up Turkey today. Especially the Roman, Byzantine and Ottoman cultures have well preserved sites representing the ancient and more recent times.

After signing the World Heritage Convention in 1983, Turkey considered the possible sites which would be eligible for nomination. Starting with 1984, files were prepared by the Ministry of Culture and submitted to UNESCO. At the moment Turkey has nine sites on the World Heritage List. The first sites nominated for inclusion to the World Heritage List were Divriği, Göreme and Istanbul. They were inscribed in the List of World Heritage in 1985. Other sites followed. Hattusha, the capital of the Hittites was included in the World Heritage List in 1986; Nemrut Dağ in 1987, Hierapolis, Xanthos and Letoon in 1988, Safranbolu in 1994, and Troy in 1998.

Although Turkey has a rich collection of natural reserves, with special flora and fauna, majority of the World Heritage sites are cultural. There is a rich range of time in the sites, spanning from prehistory through more recent times. While Troy exemplifies human habitation from prehistory, Divriği is a medieval Seljuk monument with extraordinary sculptural work and Safranbolu is a well-preserved small Ottoman town with stone monuments and timber houses dating from Ottoman period.

Turkey has not yet proposed a natural site for the List. Two of the properties on the List are mixed sites, with both cultural and natural features. There are different examples of men's intelligent use of nature; as a beautiful setting for a settlement, as places of refuge at times of oppression, as sites of recreation, seclusion or inspiration. All these possibilities are exemplified by two archaeological sites within unique natural settings: Hierapolis and Göreme.

Below the World Heritage properties of Turkey are presented in chronological order, starting with the earlier cultural properties and proceeding towards the Roman and medieval sites.

TROY

Troy, which is situated at the entrance of Dardanelles, is one of the most famous archaeological sites of the world. It is well-known due to the literary works of Homer; the Iliad and the Odyssey. The Iliad tells about the war between the Greeks and the Trojans which started because Paris, the younger son of King Priam stole Helen, the beautiful wife of the Spartan King Menelaos. In the Iliad Troy and its environs, as well as the war which lasted ten years are described in detail.

Troy is an interesting place where the eastern and western civilizations met and had interaction in the Early Bronze Age. The Trojan War was very influential and its heroes were venerated. During the Hellenistic period tumulus were erected over the supposed burial places of the heroes of the Trojan War; for Achilles, Ajax, Hector and Patroclus. Alexander the Great visited the site and promised to improve the conditions but he could not live to fulfill his wish. Romans believed that through their ancestor Aeneas they were affiliated to Troy.

The Iliad and the Odyssey, literary works created about 700 BC inspired many people, artists, writers and musicians through the centuries. Among them H. Schliemann, a German millionaire, was the one who ventured to find the treasures of King Priam. He was not an archaeologist but was interested in history. After visiting Rome and Pompei, he was fascinated with the finds and wanted to have an excavation of his own. He got interested in finding the Troy of the Iliad. Schliemann read all the sources which could provide further information about Troy. The city of King Priam had already been located at Hisarlık Tepe with the help of some small coins found in the nineteenth century. The name "New Ilion" was written on the coins. Ilion and Troy were the same city; in fact Homer referred to the city with both of its names in the Iliad.

In 1863, Frank Calvert, the American consul at Dardanelles, was also interested in doing archaeology at Troy. He had bought a piece of land and started some excavation at Hisarlık Tepe. On his first visit to the site, Schliemann talked to Calvert and learned about the potentials of the site. He made a a trial dig, excavating a deep well. For a comprehensive excavation, he applied to get permission from the Ottoman authorities. After obtaining a permit in 1871, he could start excavation.

Troy, the wooden horse erected at the site in 1973

Schliemann was aiming to get quick results; but it was not an easy site. At the top there was the Byzantine and Roman levels. The level Schliemann wanted to reach was buried deep down in the ground. To get a cross-section through the mound, he opened a wide and deep trench. By this intervention, he destroyed some walls and a lot of historic evidence. During his excavations, Schliemann found four cities at different layers under the Roman settlement of Ilium. He uncovered a defensive wall, an altar for sacrifices, a road, a gateway and a small building.

It was getting very complex as he excavated deeper down. In 1873 he found many interesting objects, which he named as the "Treasure". The find consisted of huge copper bowls, bronze, gold, silver and electron cups and a hoard of copper spearheads. There was also a group of jewellery which Schliemann named "the jewels of Helen." The collection included 8750 tiny gold rings, bracelets, sixty earrings, a head band and two diadems. He thought, he had reached the level of the Iliad, when he found the jewellery. He was mistaken in dating the level; the finds were from Troy II, which is about 1000 years earlier.

Although he had an agreement with the Ottoman authorities to share the finds, Schliemann excavated stealthily while the workers were resting or having lunch and took away the valuable finds secretly to Athens. When the news spread about the discovery of the "Treasure", Ottoman authorities

Troy, fortifications

were offended and wanted to sue Schliemann. He had to pay a fine for the finds, in order to be able to continue work. The discovery of a rich collection of ancient jewellery was an exciting news for the world. Schliemann was invited to several countries and exhibited the finds in many places. The Treasure was finally taken to Berlin. During the World War II, Berlin was occupied and the Treasure disappeared. After many years, the collection was recovered at the Pushkin Museum in Moscow and was exhibited to the public for the first time in 1998.

After H. Schliemann's death in 1890, the excavations continued with the financial support of his wife. W. Dörpfeld, a German archaeologist who had worked with Schliemann, took the lead. Dörpfeld uncovered Troy VI during the campaigns between 1893-4. The fortifications at this level had defense walls angled at the bottom, as described by Homer in his Iliad. The pottery finds helped to date the level between 1500 and 1250 BC Since the Trojan War is roughly dated to mid 13th century BC, this could be the level related to the Trojan War. There has been no agreement among the archaeologists about the finds related to a war; it is not certain if a Trojan War ever took place or it is merely fiction. Some historians claim that the rivalry between the Mycenaeans and the Trojans to control the Dardanelles was the real reason of the war.

Between 1932 and 1938, Carl W. Blegen from USA worked at the site, trying to solve problems of stratigraphy. Some conservation and restoration works were carried out during the period. The finds from his excavations are exhibited in Çanakkale and Istanbul Museums. Since late 1980's German Archaeological Institute is actively involved with the site. Professor Manfred Korfmann lead the campaigns from 1988 until his death in 2005. His research revealed that there existed a lower city outside of the walls and the city was in fact much larger in size than thought before. With international participation, efforts were channelized to improve the presentation of the ruins, to maintain the site and stop further deterioration.

At Troy, there are the physical remains of several layers of habitation. Due to its suitable position, the site was inhabited continuously for more than 3000 years. More than 50 levels of settlement have been spotted by the archaeologists. Earthquakes, wars, fires devastated the settlement several times. Several cultures, people settled over the same place, building up a mound more than 15 meters high. The lowest seven levels, called Troy I to VII, start with the Bronze Age and come up to Early Iron Age.

Troy I, dating from early Bronze Age II (app. 2920-2550 BC) had defense walls made of roughly cut stones. The plan of the settlement was roughly octagonal in plan with a major entrance gate placed at the south side. The entrance was flanked by two towers, which are rectangular in plan. A row of houses with rectangular plans were arranged on the western part of the city. Among them one had a megaron plan. The population lived on agriculture, animal husbandry and fishing. The pottery from this level has decoration in dark brown and black; there was also white incised ware.

Troy II (app. 2550-2250 BC/ Early Bronze Age II) had trade relations with far away countries. Its walls were 330 meters long and 6 m high. The walls had stone foundations and bases; the upper parts were made of adobe. There were

Troy, the lower city and the surrounding area

several structures with megaron plan; these probably served as cult buildings. The level connected with the Trojan War is Troy VI. Above the prehistoric levels, there is the Hellenistic (Troy VIII) and Roman levels (Troy IX). The Greek and Roman levels are represented by several monuments. The sanctuary complex which was probably founded in the 8th century BC was enlarged by Alexander the Great and later by Augustus. Two major public buildings survive from the Roman city, the odeion and the bouleuterion near the agora. The Byzantine Ilion, which is called Troy X is at the very top of the settlement.

Troy was included in the World Heritage List according to criteria ii, iii, and vi in 1998 as number 849. The site is evaluated as having immense significance in the understanding of the development of European civilization. It is a place where the confrontation between Anatolia and the Mediterranean world resulted in the cross cultural ties to develop in the following eras. Troy's relation with the Iliad and the influence of this important literary work on the creative arts over more than two thousand years was also noted.

Systematic excavations continue at the site under the leadership of Professor Dr. Enst Pernicka from Tübingen University, in collaboration with University of Cincinnati. Multidisciplinary studies are being carried out. The earlier findings are reviewed with the help of modern methods. The lower city is being explored systematically. Documentation of the present condition of the ruins continues. The fact that some of the surviving structures are in adobe, makes it very difficult to preserve them in the open. Maintenance and preventive conservation works are carried out to stop material degradation and loss of original fabric.

Several scientific publications are made about the site and the recent projects. The site is accessible to the visitors. Reconstitution drawings showing the development of the site through history are available, in order to enable the visitors

Troy, the Roman Odeion

to understand the site better. The Ministry of Culture and Tourism is responsible for the management of the site. To control the development around the archaeological site, a green belt has been created in the buffer zone in 1996. The National Park Department of the Ministry of Forestry collaborates with the Museum authorities to protect the area. The Long-term Development Plan for Troy National Park has been developed and put into action in 2004.

HATTUSHA: The Hittite Capital

The capital of the Hittites is located about 150 km to the east of Ankara, within the province of Çorum.

Hittites ruled in Anatolia between 1600 and 1200 BC; they were one of the superpowers of their time in the Near East. They had several cities in central and south Anatolia, extending into Syria. They had relations with Mesopotamia; they made war with the Egyptians.

Hittite Kingdom and the Hittites were forgotten in the Hellenistic and later periods. The discovery of Hattusha is relatively recent; Charles Texier, who visited the site in 1834 made drawings of the remains and published them in France. His drawings of the ruins and the reliefs at Yazılıkaya aroused great interest. By the end of the nineteenth century,

Hattusha, Lion Gate

archaeologists knew more about the Hittites and their activity in and around Asia Minor. In 1893-94 Ernest Chantre dug some trenches in the Great Temple on Büyükkale and at Yazılıkaya, discovering cuneiform tablets. In 1906 Macridy Bey from Istanbul Archaeological Museum and Hugo Winckler, a German specialist in Assyrian culture started the first systematic excavations at the site. Among the finds there was a peace treaty acted between Egyptian Pharaoh Ramses II and Hittite King Hattushili III. Concluding from the fact that such an important document would be kept at the capital city, the archaeologists decided that the site they were working on was Hattusha. They found hundreds of tablets written in Akkadian and the Hittite language, which was not known at that time. Akkadian cuneiform writing on clay tablets enabled the Hittite language to be deciphered in 1915 by Bedrich Hrozny. The study of the cuneiform tablets of Hattusha led to the birth of Hittitology as a discipline. Hattusha cuneiform tablet archives are kept in the Ankara and Istanbul archaeological museums. This rich collection amounting to 30.000 tablets was included in UNESCO's List of the Memory of the World in 2001.

Excavations revealed that the settlement around the site started as early as 6000 BC, during the Chalcolithic period.

An Assyrian colony had been established by the traders exchanging goods between Anatolia and Mesopotamia. Assyrian traders introduced writing to Anatolia in the 19th and 18th centuries BC Hittites migrated to this region and established their capital about 17th century BC The first Hittite king was Hattushili, meaning "the one from Hattusha". Twentyseven Hittite kings are known by their names. Tablets found at different sites were important in providing information about the Hittite way of life. The tablets include official Hittite correspondence and contracts, legal codes, procedures for cult ceremony.

Hattusha is situated on the slope of a high rocky massif, surrounded by steep valleys along its eastern and western sides. It measured approximately one by two kilometers. The highest point of the city is at Yerkapı which is 1240 m above the sea. There is a difference of 300 meters from the highest point to the lowest part of the city. The residence of the king was on the ridge of Büyükkale. Temples were built for the thousand gods of the Hatti Land. The city was deserted around 1200 BC parallel to the collapse of the Great Hittite Empire.

Excavations in the twentieth century by the German Archaeological Institute (DAI) revealed the urban features of the Hittite capital. The first digs took place between the years 1931-1939. There was an intermission during the World War II; excavations were resumed in 1952. Research, restoration and documentation has continued since then, bringing to light most of the city and its significant buildings. The royal palace, temples and the fortifications surrounding the upper and the lower city are important elements of the capital city. The walls and the gates of the city were studied, providing interesting details about the ancient military architecture of Anatolia. Thirty temples and several administrative buildings were identified in the upper city. The sculpture preserved at the the Lions' and Royal gates and the carvings at Yazılıkaya are exceptional rock art specimens from the second millenium BC.

The capital of Hittites was included on the World Heritage List in 1986 as number 377, according to criteria i, ii, iii and iv.

i) The city's fortifications, along with Lions' Gate and the Royal Gate and the Yazılıkaya rupestral ensemble together with its sculpted friezes, represent unique artistic achievements as monuments.

ii) Hattusha exerted dominating influence upon the civilizations of the 2nd even the 1st millenium BC in Anatolia and northern Syria.

iii) The palaces, temples, trading quarters and necropolis of this political and religious metropolis provide a

Yazılıkaya, mortuary temple reserved for the royal cult

comprehensive picture of a capital and bear a unique testimony to the disappeared Hittite civilization.

iv) Several types of buildings or architectural ensembles are perfectly preserved in Hattusha: the royal residence, the temples and the fortifications.

In recommending the inclusion of Hattusha on the World Heritage List, ICOMOS stressed the fact that this unique archaeological site, whose importance is universally recognized, will help to strengthen the credibility and representativeness of the List of the cultural properties of mankind.

Yazılıkaya, an open air sanctuary, which is regarded as the pantheon of the Hittite gods is about 2 km to the capital. It constitutes of two rooms (chambers A and B), surrounded by natural limestone walls rising up to 12 meters. The sanctuary is open to the sky; it is an open air cult area decorated with reliefs of gods carved on the natural rock surface.

Originally the rock sanctuary was screened from the outside world by an entrance building. Only the lower part of the masonry wall survives from this structure. Through this building one could enter the larger chamber A. Here on either side, a long procession of gods and goddesses are carved on the rock, within horizontal panels. The male deities are dressed with skirts and high pointed hats. They wear shoes which curl up at the toe, like the traditional hide shoes the Anatolian people wore until mid twentieth century. Many are armed with either a sword or a mace. The female deities are dressed in long pleated skirts and all wear curling toed shoes, earrings and high headdresses.

The figures all look towards the end of the chamber where the weather god and the sun goddess are depicted as standing and greeting each other. The sanctuary is regarded as the "House of the New Year's Celebration", a temple for the weather god Teshup, where festivities were held to honour all the pantheon at the coming of the New Year and the beginning of spring.

The largest relief figure which stands opposite the climatic scene, at the end of the procession of goddesses is Great King Tudhaliya IV, who was responsible for the final arrangement of the Yazılıkaya sanctuary around the middle of the 13th century BC.

The smaller chamber (B) is identified as a memorial to the Great King Tudhaliya IV, erected by his son Suppiluliuma II. The reliefs in chamber B depict the gods of the underworld. They wear short skirts and shoes curling up at the toe. Each carries a crescent shaped sword flung over the shoulder and the horned pointed hats that identify them as divinities. On the wall opposite, the divinity Sharumma, the patron of Tudhaliya IV is depicted with the Great King under his left arm. This is interpreted as patronage of the Great King in his afterlife. Next to this relief, there is another panel with an upright sword. The pommel on the hilt is shaped as a male head wearing the tall horned and pointed hat of the gods. This figure is identified as the god of the underworld. A third relief in this chamber is a cartouche with the name and title of the Great King Tudhaliya IV.

A lot of time and care has been devoted by the German Archaeological team to clear the site and present the

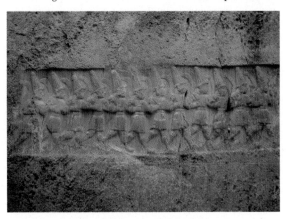

Yazılıkaya, the twelve deities in the small gallery

Hattusha, pots for grain storage at the Great Temple

remains of the Hittite Royal Citadel on Büyükkale. Large
scale excavation has exposed wide areas of the settlement
in the Lower City, the Great Temple, the temple precinct in
the upper City and its surroundings, as well as on the high
spur of Büyükkaya.

The low walls level with the ground give an idea about the
plans of the major monuments. At a site with only low walls,
reconstruction of high, full scale architectural elements is
critical. To start such a project at a World Heritage site is a risk
to the authenticity of the site. In spite of this, a reconstruction
project including a 65 meters long stretch of the city wall
was undertaken between 2003 and 2005. Two towers rising
to a height of 12 meters were reconstructed using mud brick.
The project is presented as an experimental project to draw
attention to the site and give an idea about the traditional
construction process. The attempt to assess the visual
impact of the walls in prehistoric times was maybe satisfied
but to the disadvantage of the ruins.

Hattusha, partial reconstruction of the city wall

NEMRUT DAĞ

Nemrut Dağ is a hierotheseion; a funerary monument composed of the cult center and the tumulus of the Commagene King Antiochos I (69-34 BC). It is located in southeast Turkey, 86 km to the northeast of Adıyaman. The 2206 meter high tumulus is visible from long distances.

Commagene was a small kingdom which appeared after the dissolution of the Seleucids. Its lands stretched from Euphrates in the east to Kahramanmaraş in the west and from Taurus mountains in the north to Antioch in the south. The word commagene means the combination of genes; the kingdom claimed kinship to Alexander the Great from one side and the Persian kingdom from the other. The capital of the kingdom, Samosata, is now inundated by the Atatürk Dam. The region is rich with other monuments from the same dynasty. Several funerary monuments at Kahta; a bridge and fortifications reflect the refined style and workmanship of the architecture. Commagene Kingdom was annexed to the Roman Empire in 72 AD, becoming part of Province of Syria.

The site was discovered in 1881 by Charles Sester, a German engineer. Through the expeditions of Otto Puchstein and Carl Humann in 1882-83, Nemrut Dağ was made known to the world. Due to the hardships of reaching the site, excavation was a hard undertaking. Theresa Goell worked at the site between 1954 and 1976. Documentation and archaeological studies continued in the 20th and 21st centuries with the efforts of several archaeological teams.

The hierotheseion of Antiochos is one of the most prominent and inspiring monuments of Hellenistic culture. It combines Hellenistic, Persian and Anatolian traditions. The monument at the top of the 2150m high Nemrut Dağ is dated to the first century BC It consists of a 50m high tumulus and three terraces which surround it on the east, west and north sides. The tumulus has a diameter of 140 meters and was originally 60meters high; but the small irregular stone chips which cover it have moved down and the height is diminished.

The eastern terrace which measures 21 by 26 meters is very impressive with its colossal figures seated in a row, with the spectacular tumulus rising at their back. The figures belong to the god Apollo, goddess Tyche, Zeus Oromasdes, Antiochos I and Hercules. Zeus is depicted as Oromasdes and Hercules as Artagnes, their Persian counterparts. The 7m high statues are carved in sitting position on thrones; they have stools under their feet. The heads which have very fine expressions, have fallen down. In an old photo published by Dörner, the head of Tyche is still in-situ, giving an idea about the full scale of the beautiful figure.

In contrast to the heads which are quite elaborate, the bodies are rounded, without much detail on their lower part. Figures are composed of gigantic blocks of limestone put one above the other. To work on such colossal figures at the top of a high mountain is a unique achievement in itself. Behind the figures, there is the nomos-the will of Antiochos carved on stone.

In front of the figures, there is a terrace and an altar which is described as a stepped pyramid by T. Goell. The north and south sides of the terrace are bordered by sandstone orthostats. The ones on the north side have Persian figures in low relief, signifying the Persian ancestors of Antiochos. On the south side, the Macedonian ancestors are represented. Inscriptions carved on the backs of the slabs identify the figures.

The western terrace which measures about 50 by 30 meters, has a composition similar to the eastern terrace, except the altar. Its floor is at a level about 11 meters lower than the eastern one. Five colossal statues belonging to Apollo, goddess Tyche, Zeus Oromasdes, Antiochos I and Hercules were seated between two lion-eagle figures. The bodies are not well preserved. The heads are on the ground. Antiochos is depicted with a cap in the Persian style. The orthostats have the representations of the kins of Antiochos I. The Persians are placed on the south and the Macedonians on the west side. There are three special reliefs, one showing Antiochos shaking hands with Hercules. The inscription on the panel named "the king's horoscope" gives 10 July 62-61 BC; the date when Antiochos I was made king by the Romans. These

Karakuş Tumulus, eagle figure standing at the south side

panels were made of sandstone which is not very durable. Due to severe weather conditions at the top of the mound, these plates showed signs of deterioration and were moved to the conservation laboratory established at the site.

Between the east and west terraces there is the 86 meter long North terrace. It is quite narrow and bordered by a wall with eagles standing at either end. There is a total of 42 steles and 57 bases.

Nemrut Dağ was included in the List of World Heritage in 1987 as number 448, on the basis of criteria i,iii, iv.

> i) The tomb of Antiochos I of Commagene is a unique artistic achievement. The landscaping of the natural site of Nemrut Dağ is one of the most colossal undertakings of the Hellenistic epoch (some of the stone blocks used weigh up to nine tons).

> iii) The tomb or the Herotheseion of Nemrut Dağ bears unique testimony to the civilization of the kingdom of Commagene. Antiochos I is represented in this monument as a descendant of Alexander by his mother Laodice. This semi-legendary ancestry translates in genealogical terms the ambition of a dynasty that sought to remain independent of the powers of both the East and the West.

Nemrut Dağ, eastern terrace

iv) More so than the tombs at Karakuş and Eski Kahta, the tumulus at Nemrut Dağ illustrates, through the liberal syncretism of a very original pantheon, a significant historical period. The assimilation of Zeus with Oromasdes (the Iranian god Ahura mazda), and Heracles with Artagnes (the Iranian god Verathragna) finds its artistic equivalent in an intimate mixture of Greek, Persian and Anatolian aesthetics in the statuary and the bas reliefs.

Already in 1987 ICOMOS expressed its view about the works which would take place at the site, underlining that any systematic anastylosis should be discouraged because it would seriously change the topography of the site whose beauty lies largely in the fact that the statues have been damaged and the heads are scattered amoung the large stone slabs on the terraces. There was a request that all restoration work should be preceded by specific studies to avoid excessive anastylosis.

The Ministry of Culture and Tourism is in charge of the site and protects the site with staff from the Museum of Adıyaman. The mound is surrounded by a National Park which controls the wide buffer zone necessary to preserve the character of the site. A management plan for the World

Nemrut Dağ, head of Zeus on the western terrace

Heritage site and the surrounding area is being developed by the Ministry of Culture. A scientific committe was established to monitor the site. Research on the stability of the statues and terraces as well as the deterioration processes of the limestone and sandstone sculptural elements is going on. Protection measures to safeguard the delicate elements exposed to extreme weather conditions are being developed by expert team from Middle East Technical University.

XANTHOS and LETOON

Xanthos and Letoon are two ancient sites located in Lycia, southwestern Turkey. Xanthos was the capital and Letoon the cult center of Lycians. The two cities are about four kilometers apart, separated by Xanthos stream (modern Eşen). Today, Xanthos which is located on the eastern side of the river is within the Kaş municipality of Antalya, while Letoon is administratively attached to the Fethiye municipality, within Muğla province. Rock-cut tombs, pillar tombs and pillar mounted sarcophagi were characteristic burial forms of Lycia.

XANTHOS

Xanthos means yellow in ancient Greek. The foundation of the city goes back to the end of the eighth century BC It was the ancient capital of Lycia and resisted the Persian invasion in 546 BC According to historian Herodotos, Xanthians did not surrender but defended their city to the end; continuing to fight until all were killed. After this catastrophy, the city was rebuilt by families which were not in the city during the war.

Xanthos had close relations with Athens in the fourth century BC but it came to the end when the Athenean commandor Melesandros wanted to impose new taxes on the city. At the end of the fourth century BC, Alexander the Great conquered Asia Minor and Xanthos became part of his empire in 334 BC.

In the second century BC Xanthos became the capital of the Lycian League. This continued until the first century AD, when Asia Minor became part of the Roman Empire. Xanthos was taken over by the Romans in 42 BC, as a result of which the city was remodeled and several important monuments were erected. During early Byzantine period, Xanthos became the seat of a bishop. Several monuments from the Byzantine period are to be seen in the city. The city lost its dynamism after the Arab raids in the seventh century AD; becoming totally deserted in the twelfth century.

After centuries of oblivion, Xanthos and its beautiful monuments attracted attention in the nineteenth century. Charles Fellows visited Xanthos in 1838. He came again later to excavate and collect inscriptions, sculpture and architectural elements for the British Museum. The results of his excavation were published in Travels in Lycia. He chose three important tombs: the Nereid Monument, the Harpy tomb and the tomb of Payava. The architectural pieces were transferred to England and reassembled in the British Museum. The Nereid Monument, the Harpy Tomb and Payava sarcophagus dating from 370-360 BC are now presented to the public in London.

Systematic excavations in the twentieth century by French professors P. Demarque and H. Metzger were concentrated

Xanthos, Harpy monument and the Lycian tomb

at the Lycian acropolis. Their work revealed the ancient Lycian city dating from the sixth and fifth centuries BC Recent excavations lead by Prof. J. Des Courtils brought to light more elements of the city center; two main streets, two squares and a basilica from the second century AD The ruins at Xanthos can be examined in two sections. The first is the Lycian Acropolis, the rocky area rising over the Xanthos River. The ruling kings of Xanthos built their monumental tombs on the acropolis of the city. There were several kinds of burial but two types of funerary buildings are special. The so called "pillar tombs" are composed of a base supporting a burial chamber. The walls of the chamber could be decorated with reliefs. The other type is the "pillar mounted sarcophagus." Such tombs consist of a stone base with a stone sarcophagus above. Just like Etruscans, Lycians built tombs in the shape of houses. Sarcophagus tombs were carved in stone but imitated the details of timber architecture. It is interesting to note that the timber architecture of the region has come to our day. The rural people of the area construct houses and granaries in the same technique as is observed in the tombs.

The earliest surviving tombs in Xanthos were pillar tombs. The tomb of Kybernis, King of Xanthos, constructed about 480 BC is a fine example of this type. The tomb is known as the "Harpy tomb" due to the four female figures at the corners. The tomb chamber with fine reliefs on its walls was raised on a great pillar of dark limestone weighing around 80 tons. The whole structure stood about nine meters high. The top of the chamber was covered by a flat slab of stone which projected from the walls, forming eaves like a roof.

The most impressive tomb of Xanthos was the Nereid Monument, from which only the foundations are left behind. Around 400 BC Arbinas ordered a mausoleum for himself in Greek style. Architectural features of this monument were borrowed from the Erechteion at the acropolis of Athens.

Xanthos, Tomb of Payava

Xanthos, Nereid Monument

The fifth century BC walls of Xanthos were constructed using the polygonal technique, a fact which reflects Greek influence. The city walls which are more than two kilometers long, were extended and restored several times.

The most imposing monument at Xanthos is the theater, which was founded during the Hellenistic period and renovated by the Romans. Next to the theater there is the Lycian tomb standing over a pedestal and the Harpy monument. The stele at the northeast corner of the agora is an important monument with an inscription in the Lycian language. Lycian alphabeth was basically Greek, with some additional characters; the texts can be read but the language has not yet been deciphered.

LETOON

Letoon is related to Leto, who was the mother of Apollo and Artemis. Zeus had an affair with her and she had twin babies. According to Greek mythology, while escaping from the wrath of Hera, the jealous wife of Zeus, she came to Lycia. She hid herself and the babies near a water spring. Letoon became the cult center of the Lycians. To honour Leto, people of Letoon built three temples, dedicated to Leto, Artemis and Apollo. The temple dedicated to Leto is built in Ionian style and dated to the end of the fifth century BC The small temple next to it is dedicated to Artemis and dates from the fourth century BC The third temple, which is in Doric style belonged to Apollo. The celebrations of the Lycian League took place here and the priests of the place had high positions as its religious leaders.

An inscription dated 358 BC was found close to the temple of Artemis. Its text written in three languages: Lycian, Old Greek and Aramaic. The inscription was a decree made to the satrap of Caria and Lycia. The long Lycian texts carved on rocks or in the form of huge monoliths are regarded as monuments of the Lycian language, a unique Indo-European language that has disappeared a long time ago.

There is a nymphaeum to the southwest of the temples. It was built at the site of the sacred spring that was associated with Leto. To the north of the temples, there are the remains of the Hellenistic and Roman porticos. In the northeast part of Letoon, there is a Roman theater. From the Byzantine period, there is the rest of a fifth century church.

The recent history of the site has parallels with Xanthos. It was discovered by European travellers in the nineteenth century. O. Benndorf visited the site in 1840. Systematic excavations were started in 1962 by French archaeologists.

Letoon, temples dedicated to Leto, Artemis and Apollo

Prof. H. Metzger revealed three temples, the round portico and the L planned stoa. Hundreds of incriptions and ceramics which date back to the eighth century BC were found. The most famous of the incriptions is the one in three languages which dates from the fourth century BC The site was deserted after the seventh century.

ICOMOS evaluation in May 1988, recognized the originality of the tombs at Xanthos and Letoon; the report pointed out to the fact that pillar tombs and pillar mounted sarcophagi represent a novel type of funerary architecture. It was also stressed that the rich series of Lycian tombs at Xanthos and Letoon made it easy to understand the successive acculturation phenomena that took place in Lycia from the sixth century BC.

The two sites were included on World Heritage List in 1988 on the basis of criteria ii and iii.

> ii) Xanthos directly influenced Lycia throughout Antiquity, as can be seen for example at the archaeological sites of Patara or Pınara. However, it also considerably influenced the neighboring provinces. The Halicarnassus Mausoleum, which the Ancients ranked as one of the Seven Wonders of the World, is a direct descendant of Xanthos' Nereid Monument.

Letoon, porticos affected by rising of groundwater

iii) Xanthos and Letoon bear exceptional testimony to the Lycian civilization both through the many epigraphic texts found on the 2 sites as well as by the remarkable funerary monuments preserved there or originating from the area.

The two sites are surrounded by wide agricultural areas. Agricultural pressure is felt especially around Letoon. The green houses have a negative effect on the surrounding landscape. The seasonal rising of the groundwater table affects the monuments in Letoon. A management plan, including environmental control and a study of the preservation of the monuments in both sites is needed.

HİERAPOLİS

Hierapolis is an ancient city located 18 kilometers to the northeast of Denizli. It is situated high up on a hill, overlooking the Lycos valley of Phrygia. The site is famous for its hot water springs and spectacular travertine hills which are above the plateau where the modern Pamukkale village is located. The Turkish name of the site: Pamukkale, meaning 'the cotton castle', was inspired by the foamy white hillside created as a result of the sedimentation of hot calcerous water coming down the cliff.

The curative properties of the hot water were appreciated far back in Antiquity. The hot water is rich in calcium hydrocarbonate as it comes out of the spring. When it gets in touch with the outside air, it cools down and the precipitation settles down on the ground. The site is unique and has exceptional beauty with the formation of shallow pools and sequences of cascades down the slope.

Hierapolis means the 'Holy City', yet there is also another explanation to the origin of the name. The city is claimed to be established by the Pergamon King Eumenes II, in 190 BC Thus it is related to Hiera, queen of the Amazons and the wife of Telephus, the legendary founder of the Pergamon Kingdom. The 2nd century BC inscriptions found at the site confirm the alleged date of the city's foundation.

Hierapolis went under Roman rule in 129 BC and was embellished with several impressive monuments. Due to recurring damages by earthquakes, the city had to undergo restoration several times. Two big earthquakes occurred in 17 and 60 AD The extent of destruction after the earthquake in 60 AD made it necessary to reconstruct the city. The Asian Proconsul Sextus Julius Frontinus was assigned to carry out the works. During the reign of Emperor Domitian (r. 81–96 AD), the city was extended outside of the walls, in the northern direction. An enormous agora (280x170 m), a theater, and the bath which is turned into a basilica in the Byzantine period were part of this expansion.

Due to its importance, the city was visited by several of the Roman emperors; by Hadrian in 129, by Caracalla in 215 and by Valens in 370. Most of the major monuments, like the thermal baths, nymphaeums, the theater were constructed during the 2nd and 3rd centuries AD The good quality of the marble decoration and the scale of the constructions are proof of the ample sources of funds available for the city.

Today most of the urban features are from the Roman period. The elements of the Hellenistic city could not survive the ravages of time and the tremors. According to the results of excavations, the city spread over an area roughly measuring

Hierapolis, a tumulus type tomb from the western necropolis

1000x800 m. The fact that several of the major monuments are still standing in their full height, makes the site very impressive. Due to topographical reasons, the main direction of the growth was in the north-south axis. Between the north and south gates runs the main street of the city; it is about 1 km long and divides the city into two. The main street was extended to the north and south and were connected to new gateways. Of the two, only the northern gate, which consists of a triple arch flanked by two round towers survives. The inscription gives the name of Emperor Domitian and is dated to 84-85 AD

During the excavations to the east and west of the main street, the urban grid system of the city was revealed. Narrow streets surround the insulae; the remains of houses and other buildings are preserved and presented to the visitors. Information about the citizens of Hierapolis is gathered from the inscriptions in the necropolis. It was a cosmopolitan city with native Anatolians, Greeks, Romans and Jews. Woollen industry, including dying, washing and carpet weaving were very lively in Hierapolis. Guilds like nail makers, coppersmiths were recorded among the craftsmen of the city.

Hierapolis, cascades

The baths were among the most imposing buildings of the city. They had large pools with hot water supplied from the springs nearby. Hydrotherapy was an important service provided by the place. The gymnasium-palaestra complex in the center is partially preserved. A section of the building is restored and used as the site museum. The second major bath, called the Bath-Basilica was converted into a church in the fifth century. It has suffered severely from earthquake damage; some of its tilted and cracked walls and vaults are still standing.

Hierapolis is located on the Meander fault line; occasionally fumes come out of certain cracks in the ground. In ancient times, the volcanic character of the soil was associated to god Pluto, the lord of the underworld. In Hierapolis there was a Plutonium, a grotto which emitted poisonous fumes. Recent excavations have revealed the remnants of the Temple Apollo; the principal deity of Hierapolis was built next to the Plutonium. Due to natural factors, the Hellenistic temple was renovated in the third century AD and suffered from another earthquake in the fifth century.

The population of the city increased considerably during the second and third centuries. Christianity reached the city at the end of the fourth century. St. Philip lived here and was

Hierapolis, Bath-Basilica

prosecuted in 87. Several churches were erected in the city during the Byzantine period. The town became a bishopric in the 4th and 5th centuries. Some Roman buildings, like the bath near the northern entrance to the city, were adapted to serve for the new religion. In the sixth century, during the reign of Justinian, Hierapolis was promoted to the rank of metropolitan.

With its cathedral, baptisterium and churches, Hierapolis has a good collection of important monuments from the early Christian period. The martyrium of St. Philip is an outstanding funerary monument from the fifth century. Situated at a location overlooking the city, it has been a new focus of attention for the city. The monument measures 20x20 m from outside; at its core, there is an octagonal courtyard, surrounded by rooms and recesses. The martyrion attracted many visitors; it was used for commemorative services and the recital of panegyrics on the saint's feast day. A christian quarter developed around it in time. Recently, archaeologists have discovered an octagonal building close to the martyrion. It is presumed to be a baptisterium, probably used by pilgrims who demanded to be baptized before visiting the tomb of St. Philip.

Foreign travellers started to visit Hierapolis in the 19th century. The first researches were conducted by a German

82   Hierapolis, northern gate with triple arch and round towers

expedition, lead by C. Humann, at the end of the nineteenth century. After a long period of intermission, Italian archaeologists directed by Professor P. Verzone from the Polytechnic of Torino started to work at the site. Since 1957, the Italian Archaeological Mission including archaeologists, architects and other scientists from universities of Torino, Lecce, Venice and Milano has been active at the site. Due to the two meters high petrified calcerous deposits over the historic center, excavation was not an easy task.

The northern necropolis which covers an area longer than two kilometers has been excavated, revealing closely spaced tombs. The necropolis of Hierapolis shows a wide variation of funerary traditions. Tombs range in date from late Hellenistic to early Christian times. The inscriptions provide details about the social status, ethnicity, identity and provenance of the buried people. Many of the tombs consist of a solid base on which were set one or more sarcophagi. Others are larger and more impressive. The tumuli add to the variety of the tombs. They comprise a low circular wall at the base with a cone of earth above, surmounted by a phallus stone or another emblem. In the interior, there is a funeral chamber with stone benches for the dead.

Hierapolis, a restored tomb

The theater of Hierapolis is a magnificient monument dating from the period of Emperor Severus (r. 193-211); it probably replaced an earlier Flavian structure at the same spot. The position of the theater commands a nice view over the city. Besides classical performances, the theater was used for gladiatorial and wild beast shows. An inscription in the wall of the diazoma greets Hierapolis as " Foremost land of broad Asia, mistress of nymphs, adorned with streams of water and all beauty".

The podium of the scaenae frons was decorated with a figurative cycle dedicated to Apollo and Artemis. The sculpture is very refined and shows influence of Aphrodisias school. The upper part of the scaenae had collapsed. Hundreds of architectural blocks scattered around were surveyed and classified to develop a reconstitution drawing of the three tiered scaenae frons. The structural problems of the theater were inspected and treated; at present it is in quite good condition and is very impressive as the largest intact structure of the city.

Hierapolis was included on the List of World Heritage in 1988 on the basis of criteria iii and iv.

Hierapolis, Martyrion of St. Philip

iii) Hierapolis is an exceptional example of a Greco-Roman thermal installation expressly established on an extraordinary natural site. The therapeutic virtues of the waters were exploited at the various thermal installations which included immense hot basins and pools for swimming. Hydrotherapy was accompanied by religious practices, which were developed in relation to local cults. The Temple of Apollo, which includes Chthonian divinities, was erected on a fault from which noxious vapors escaped. The theatre, which dates from the time of Severus, is decorated with an admirable frieze depicting a ritual procession and a sacrifice to the Ephesian Artemis. The necropolis, which extends over 2 kilometers, affords a vast panorama of the funerary practices of the Greco-Roman epoch.

iv) The Christian monuments of Hierapolis, erected between the 4th and the 6th centuries, constitutes an outstanding example of an early Christian architectural group with a cathedral, baptistry and churches. The most important monument, situated outside the northwest wall of the city, is the martyrium of St. Philip. At the top of a monumental stairway, the octagonal layout of the building is remarkable because of its ingenious spatial organization. Radiating from the central octagon are chapels, polygonal halls and triangular rooms which combine to culminate in a square structure encircled by rectangular cells bordered with porticoes.

Due to its outstanding natural properties, Hierapolis became a natural-cultural site, with the addition of criteria vii (earlier natural iii). The travertine terraces with 20 m high cliffs and waterfalls, situated along the foothill of Çökelez mountains was found important in relation to the site's historic and cultural associations. A management plan for the protection of the landscape and the environment was found crucial.

After more than 50 years of excavations, major monuments of the city, the cathedral, Martyrion of St. Philip, Temple of Apollo, the theater were researched, the tombs in the northern necropolis were revealed. The restoration of the Frontinus street and other urban elements has improved the visual impact of the ancient center. Cleaning and conservation works conducted in the theater improved its integrity and outlook; it is occasionally used for performances.

The Ministry of Culture and Tourism is in charge of the site. A small local museum was created in the big bath complex, to exhibit some of the interesting objects found in the excavations. During the recent years, the hotels which had crouched on the travertines were removed. A new landscaping has been developed to improve the presentation of the site. The Turkish law on cultural heritage was amended in 2004 in order to enable the Ministry of Culture and Tourism to develop management plans for cultural sites. Each year about two million tourists visit the site. This brings a lot of pressure on the site. To maintain such a large site which welcomes so many visitors requires a lot of trained guards and conservation staff. The site is monitored by experts from the local museum, universities and NGO's; conservation efforts will continue to improve the conditions

Hierapolis, theater

to preserve both the archaeological and the natural elements of Hierapolis.

Hierapolis was destroyed by several earthquakes in history; the marks of earthquakes are visible on several of the monuments. The idea to present the site as a seismo-archaeological park has been proposed by Professor F. D'Andria who is directing the Italian Archaeological Mission at the moment. The intention is to keep the interventions to the monuments the minimum, so that the impact of earthquakes will continue to be visible. Thus it will be possible to preserve the seismic history of the site as it is reflected on the monuments. This kind of approach is of crucial importance in order to preserve the authenticity and integrity of the site. With this principle in mind, the Italian Archaeological Mission developed a project to preserve the endangered Bath-Basilica. A modern buttressing system was designed to hold the out of plumb wall of the Bath-Basilica in place, without intervening too much with its earthquake affected condition.

GÖREME NATIONAL PARK AND THE ROCK SITES OF CAPPADOCIA

Cappadocia is located in central Anatolia. It is a wide area with a spectacular landscape, carved out of tuff and andesitic material by the action of water and wind. The creation of soft, undulating forms as a result of erosion over millenia is a unique natural phenomenon. The differential erosion of volcanic tuff sediments has resulted in the creation of conical elements topped by big blocks. These are called "fairy chimneys" in Turkish, reflecting the spirit of the picturesque, dream like landscape within which they are found Human settlement at central Anatolia goes back to prehistoric times; historic levels include the Hittites, Romans, Byzantines and Seljuks. The cultural landscape of Cappadocia was created by man's patient work on the rock, carving it for religious and civil buildings. It is believed that the first signs of monastic activity in Cappadocia date back to the fourth century. Christians, who escaped from massacre or attacks looked for refuge in the Göreme valley; worked on the soft stone, carving their living spaces in the rock. In order to resist Arab attacks during the eighth and beginning of the nineth centuries, the inhabitants of the region took refuge in troglodyte villages or subterranean towns such as Kaymaklı and Derinkuyu. The underground settlements were hidden from sight and offered good protection to the local population.

The rock-hewn churches of Cappadocia are regarded as a unique record of the Early Middle Ages and the Byzantine tenth century. The monuments are very important to understand the Christianization of the region, the stylistic changes which took place during the Middle Ages and the characteristics of the rural and monastic cohabitation.

During the Iconoclast period (725-842), the decoration of the sanctuaries were restricted to the minimum; mostly to sculpted or tempera painted crosses. After 842, the churches were richly decorated with figurative painting. There are quite a number of the richly decorated churches within the Göreme Valley.

French travellers started visiting the region in the eighteenth century. After P. Lucas published his travel diary in 1714, attention was drawn to this unknown territory. J.H. Hamilton, W.F. Ainsworth and C. Texier were among the nineteenth century visitors. With their publications, interest was aroused in many others to come and see the enchanting landscape full of interesting spaces and forms. During his expedition to Cappadocia in the first half of the twentieth century, G. de Jerphanion investigated thirty seven monuments in the region. With more research, the number is now increased to 57.

At present twenty-six underground settlements have been discovered and studied within the Cappadocia region. The researchers believe that there is possibility to have more and continue their investigations. Two of the many, Kaymaklı and Derinkuyu settlements are spectacular with several floors cut deep into the rock. Piers carved cut out of solid rock support the flat or vaulted ceilings of the floors. Interesting ventilation systems, dark rooms give an idea about the living conditions in these spaces.

In 1985, part of Cappadocia, including Göreme National Park and the Cappadocian rock sites were inscribed in the List of World Heritage as item 357, according to criteria i,iii,v and vii.

> i) Owing to their quality and density, the rupestral sanctuaries of Cappadocia constitute a unique artistic achievement offering irreplacable testimony to post-iconoclast period Byzantine art.

> iii) The rupestral dwellings, villages, convents and churches retain the fossilized image as it were, of a province of Byzantine Empire between the 4th century and the Turkish invasion. Thus, they are the essential vestiges of a civilization which has disappeared.

> v) Cappadocia is an outstanding example of a traditional human settlement which has become vulnerable under the combined effects of natural erosion and, more recently, tourism.

Göreme valley was nominated as a mixed cultural/natural site. For natural properties, the following criteria were met:

> i) Outstanding example representing earth's evolutionary history. The nearby Erciyes Dağ volcano is still active and the tuff deposits it has created in the past are vivid evidence of previous volcanic activity.

> ii) On going geological processes. The eroded landscape patterns are spectacular examples of the effects of weathering processes on the underlying tuff deposits.

> iii) Superlative natural features and exceptional combinations of natural and cultural elements.

The World Heritage site of Göreme National Park and the Rock Sites of Cappadocia covers a large area within Nevşehir and Kayseri provinces. The Göreme National Park, Derinkuyu and Kaymaklı subterranean cities, Karain, Karlık, Yeşilöz villages are within Nevşehir province; the old settlement of Soğanlı village is within Kayseri's Yeşilhisar township. Göreme National Park covers Ürgüp and Avanos. An area of 9576 hectares was designated as a National Park in 1986 in order to protect the natural and archaeological assets of the region. The eastern part of the Göreme valley was turned into an open air museum by the Ministry of Culture and Tourism. Chapel of St. Basileos, churches of Elmalı, Çarıklı, Tokalı, Karanlık, Yılanlı and St. Barbara are among the important constituents of this museum.

Several missions were carried out by UNESCO and ICCROM to preserve the major churches. Photogrammetric surveys were made by the Restoration Department of the Middle East Technical University (METU), to have good documentation prior to conservation treatments. ICCROM trained a competent restoration team, several churches were restored; two under ICCROM's direct guidance and control.

The first international mission for the conservation and restoration of the mural paintings took place in 1973. With

Cappadocia, eroding tuffs

contribution of experts from ICCROM, METU and the Ministry of Culture and Tourism, the campaign lasted until 1990. Between 1973 and 1980, the conservators worked in Tokalı Church, fixing the detached plasters and conserving the murals. Between 1981 and 1990 the wall paintings of Karanlık, Elmalı, Kızlar, Kılıçlar, El Nazar and Saklı churches were treated.

Several rock hewn churches in the Göreme Valley are affected by instability problems. In the churches that are located near slopes, large cracks appear as a result of the loosening of the rock mass. The process of erosion and cracking causes great damage to the churches which are cut into the rock. Since the cracked rocks tend to collapse, it is important to take preventive measures to stop the losses to significant natural elements and cultural heritage.

El Nazar, which is one of the medieval churches in the Göreme valley, suffered from damages caused by climatic and hydrogeological factors. The domed structure was carved into a free standing conical rock. The thin walls of the apse and the entrance had been lost. The floor of the church was broken and the dome over the central space of the church was not in a safe position after losing one of its main supports. The advanced level of damages could lead to serious losses. In 1987, the Ministry of Culture and Tourism initiated a project to identify the measures for the structural consolidation of the church. A project was developed in 1989 at Istanbul Technical University by a team lead by Prof. M. Yorulmaz. The Ministry of Culture and Tourism implemented the project in 1997

Zelve, which consists of three valleys is another open air museum within the Göreme National Park. It has been an important religious center during the nineth- thirteenth centuries. Churches of Direkli, Balıklı, Üzümlü and Geyikli are among the important monuments in this part of the World Heritage Site. Soğanlı valley which constitutes of two parts is also within the World Heritage site. Several spaces, rooms and chapels decorated with frescoes have been carved into the conical rocks and also the steep walls of the valley.

Rocky sites in Cappadocia have been developed as small settlements in late Ottoman period, by building houses next to some caves. Ortahisar, Uçhisar and Çavuşin are urban sites with many houses and other facilities. These small settlements are designated and are under protection as urban sites. Recent habitation from the last centuries is in the form of houses, mosques, churches, fountains, granaries and other buildings like pigeon cotes which were essential for urban or rural life. Due to the threats arising from geological problems, cracks or rock collapses, some districts were declared as natural disaster areas and evacuated. There are also areas which were deserted because of the exchange of population between Turkey and Greece. To save the cultural heritage of Cappadocia, to preserve the integrity of historic settlements, there is need to repair and rehabilitate the abandoned and ruined areas.

Conservation plans were commissioned by the Ministry of Culture and Tourism for several of the historic urban areas in Cappadocia. A regional Commission for the Preservation of Cultural Property was established at Nevşehir to facilitate the review of restoration projects and to take decisions for immediate action when needed. Some financial assistance was provided to Cappadocia through UNESCO's International Campaign to save Istanbul and Göreme. This budget was allocated to the establishment of a GIS based inventory of the World Heritage site.

Funding for conservation and protection of the urban and archaeological areas is provided from different sources; from the state, municipalities, foundations and individuals as private owners. Recently a conservation project was initiated in Ürgüp to revive a deserted quarter of the settlement. Ürgüp is a large town within a densely built conservation area. It was an important religious center during the Byzantine period, with the seat of a bishop. It continued developing through the Seljuk and Ottoman periods.

The Kayakapı Cultural and Natural Environment Conservation and Rehabilitation Project aims to restore a historic section of the town and use it for touristic purposes. The project which was initiated in 2002 is a private investment but with legal and administrative support from the local government. The positive efforts at Kayakapı have attracted the attention of UNESCO, which has contributed to the project by sponsoring the conservation of the Kayakapı Church. Kayakapı project was developed and implemented by KA. BA Architecture, with funding from VASCO Tourism

Decorated façade of a house carved into the rock for pigeons

firm. The same architectural firm, lead by architect Cengiz Kabaoğlu, prepared the project and restored the Sarıca Church located in Mustafapaşa, Ürgüp. The medieval church is dated roughly between the 10th and 13th centuries. It suffered from infiltration of water, cracking. The project involved the restoration of wall paintings, the construction of a new drainage system and renewal of the eroded façade with natural stone. The project was awarded the Europa Nostra Award in 2007.

Since 1990's, number of visitors to Cappadocia have increased as a result of which the number of hotels has increased. There are risks arising from the pressure of development; tourism investments which do not care about the landscape are a great risk to the integrity of the site. It is evident that mass tourism is not appropriate to Cappadocia. The increase in the number of people creates serious problems of erosion on the rock surfaces. Control of tourist activities to avoid voluntary or involuntary damage to paintings and architectural details has to be achieved.

Cappadocian landscape with a so called fairy chimney and caves carved into the rc

Maintenance and preventive structural consolidation is essential. In the isolated and unguarded churches there is danger of disintegration from vandalism and natural agents. In the guarded but heavily visited churches the paintings are attacked by the visitors, humidity and direct abrasion when no barrier exists. Basic maintenance, especially in relation to mural paintings is needed. There are not enough full time employed specialists at the site. The monitoring of the damages should be followed and local conservation, implementation and monitoring units have to be established.

Ministry of Culture has taken the effort to regulate the surrounding of the Göreme Open Air Museum with car park, services and shopping facilities; yet the visitor management in the World Heritage areas needs to be improved. Visitor centers are needed to inform the tourists about the sites; the presentation and conservation of the sites have to be improved.

HISTORIC AREAS OF ISTANBUL

With its long history, Istanbul has an important place among the ancient cities of the world. Its position on the strait between Asia and Europe is an unmatched location. Being the capital of empires ruling around the Mediterranean has given Istanbul the chance to foster science and arts, along with vigor in building activity. The strife for excellence in the field of architecture was not reserved to limited periods of time; with the support of political and financial means, Istanbul has been a place where top quality designs were produced without interruption over a period of more than thousand years.

Old Istanbul is located on a peninsula, surrounded by the Golden Horn, the Bosphorus and the Marmara Sea. The major part of its population lived within the area surrounded by the land and sea walls until the end of the nineteenth century. Other historic parts of the city are Galata, the medieval settlement on the northern part of the Golden Horn; Eyüp district which developed after the fifteenth century outside of the walls, to the west of the Historic Peninsula; Scutari, the Ottoman settlement on the Asian side and the villages along the Bosphorus.

Istanbul has been a part of the Mediterranean World since ancient times with its commercial, cultural, administrative links. The site of old Istanbul, the area contained within the city walls is called the Historic Peninsula. The topography of the peninsula has made it possible to develop a city with a spectacular siting, using the accents of hilltops and the advantages of the shores. As a result, the city became an open air museum where monuments like the Hagia Sophia which is a landmark in architectural history of the world and impressive Ottoman complexes from the fifteenth to the ninetenth century dominate the skyline.

Urban history of Istanbul

The foundation of many cities are connected with some mythological figures. Istanbul also has a mtyhological beginning. According to Greek mtythology, Zeus was in love with beautiful Io. To protect her from the wrath of his consort Hera, Zeus put Io in disguise, transforming her into a white cow. Nevertheless, Hera learned about the affair and sent gadflies to annoy Io. Horrified, Io ran away with excitement to and fro ; the trajectory of her escape defined the Bosphorus. Io was pregnant and she gave birth to a girl named Keroessa, after passing the Golden Horn. Later Keroessa married Poseidon, the god of the sea and they had a son, Byzas, who grew up and lived in Megara, Greece. During his visit to the oracle in Delphi, Byzas was told to go and found a city across Chalcedon, "the country of the blind". He sailed out and travelled north from Megara, passing through the Dardanelles and reaching the entrance of the Bosphorus. As he approached the Historic Peninsula, he saw the settlement on the Asian side of the strait, presently Kadıkoy, and decided that people who settled on the Asian side, while there was a much superior place on the European side, must be considered "blind". So he settled at the tip of the promontory across Chalcedon; the colony he established was named Byzantion, after him.

The foundation of Byzantion is dated to seventh century BC The Hellenistic colony developed over the first hill of the Historic Peninsula and along the Golden Horn shore. Its economy depended on fishing, agriculture and taxes imposed on ships travelling through the Bosphorus. No physical remains of Byzantion are visible above ground today; some coins, steles are the finds obtained from excavations.

Istanbul, skyline of the Historic Peninsula from the north

Buildings and monuments were covered by the constructions of the later cultural strata.

Byzantion was pressed by Roman power at the end of the second century AD Septimius Severus sieged the city but the city would not surrender at once. The resistance against the Roman army angered Septimius Severus. After the takeover, he set the city on fire and destroyed its walls. Later he tried to make up for the destruction. Under Roman rule, Byzantion flourished; monumental buildings fitting the grandeur of the Empire entered the urban scene.

The decision of Constantine the Great to make Byzantion the capital of the Roman Empire was a great decision and a turning point in the history of the city. The capital city was enlarged, enclosing an additional 6 km square area for new settlement and public buildings. New walls were built and the city was called Nea Roma/New Rome or Constantinopolis, Constantine's city. To draw parallels with ancient Rome, which had seven hills, Constantinopolis was also organized in a way to have seven hills.

Families from Rome were invited to settle at the new capital. To embellish the city in accordance with its stature, interesting objects were brought from different parts of the Empire. The inauguration ceremony of the town took place on 11 May 330. The Hippodrome with its surviving monuments, the Aqueduct of Valens, the colossal capitals standing in the second courtyard of Topkapı Palace, the gigantic Medusa heads reused in the Basilica Cistern give an idea about the monumentality of the Roman architecture in the city.

Since the city was founded on a peninsula with the mainland in the west, its growth had to be in the westward direction. With each enlargement of the city, new defense lines were needed. The expansion of the settled area in the fourth century, under Constantine the Great, was in such a way as to include the five hills of the peninsula. Since there are no visible remains of the Constantinian wall, its exact line and features are difficult to surmise. Generally, there is an opinion that the wall started near the Marmara shore of Psammatia, advanced towards the north, uphill, passing through Ese Kapı at Cerrahpaşa, then descended down to Lycos valley, went up the hill to Fatih and reached Unkapanı on the Golden Horn.

Information about the layout of the city during the Roman period is rather schematic. Before becoming Constantinopolis, the western boundary of the city was approximately at a place where the Constantine's Column stands today. Outside the walls, there was the necropolis of the ancient city. Constantine enlarged the city and built important monuments. He established the first Hagia Sophia at the same place where the present Hagia Sophia stands. To the south of the major church, there was the forum of Augusteion. A colonnaded street, called Mese ran from the Augusteion to the west, reaching the Forum of Constantine. Although the form of the Constantinian forum is no longer discernible, there are descriptions about its original design. The forum was circular in plan, to look like the ocean. It was paved with marble slabs; in the middle rose the 50 m high porphyry

Hippodrome, base of the obelisk with Emperor Arcadius holding a wreath in his hand to give to the champion charioteer

column, topped with the bronze statue of the Emperor. The statue originally belonged to god Helios; only his head was changed to look like the Emperor. During its long history the porphyry column suffered from fires and was braced by iron rings, thereby acquiring the name Çemberlitaş in Turkish (the column with rings).

The eastern and western gates of the forum were adorned with statues. The level of the ground rose considerably in time and the surrounding urban texture was completely changed. But the basic road structure of the ancient city has survived through the centuries. The significance of the Mese, as the main thoroughfare of the city continued during the Ottoman period. The name became Divanyolu during the Ottoman period. It was used by the sultan for processions, as he and his retinue moved out from the Topkapı Palace and advanced towards the main gate of the city at Edirnekapı to start campaigns in the western direction.

A large Corinthian capital with masks in the abacus zone

A reused frize block with a Medusa head from the Basilica Cistern

From the Forum of Constantine, the colonnaded street was extended towards the west, reaching the Constantinian wall. Several other forums were established on the main axis of the town. The Forum of Theodosius was located about where the Bayezıt Square is located today. The remains of the monumental arch of Theodosius were discovered in 1957-58 during the excavations for the wide road constructed between Bayezıt and Aksaray.

A reconstitution drawing of the Theodosian Arch was made by Prof. R. Naumann, from the German Archaeological Institute, using the information from the architectural evidence discovered in situ and the marble blocks scattered around the foundations. The form and design of the 10.5 m tall gigantic columns are very special. The shafts had reliefs carved on their shaft, making these structural elements look like tree trunks. The central part of the monument was about 21 metres high, creating a very impressive image in the center of the city. Forum Bovis was the next public space on the main road. The forum of Arcadius was located to the southwest of the city, close to the Constantinian wall.

The shape of the ancient forums were changed in later times, some of the monuments standing in their middle were disturbed by earthquakes or suffered from fires. The urban fabric was changed in the Ottoman period; some of the columns lost their public appearance, becoming enclosed in the garden of private houses. One of them is the Column of Arcadius which originally stood in the middle of the Arcadius Forum. The monument has been seriously damaged by earthquakes and fires. According to some drawings from the Ottoman period, the column had fine carvings over its shaft, arranged in a band surrounding it in the form of a spiral. Inside the column, a stairway lead to the top. Today only the lower part of the monument is preserved; it stands in the garden of a private house and not visible from the street.

During the eighteenth century, the column of Marcian was also standing in the garden of a house. After the 1912 fire which devastated a large portion of the Fatih district, a new street plan was adopted. The planner for the region appreciated the value of this ancient monument and used it as the centerpiece of a new circus. Today the column stands at a crossing; with several streets directed towards it, the monument is visible from long distances.

In the fifth century, a new fortification was built by prefect Anthemious to protect the city from the assaults of the approaching Huns. This defense line is called the Theodosian Wall and is combined with sea walls on the Marmara shore and Golden Horn walls on the north. With the death of Attila, Huns did not start the expected campaign towards Constantinople, but the Theodosian Wall with its triple defence system consisting of the ditch, front wall and the main wall, has been very helpful in defending the city against other armies.

The city was embellished with civil and religious buildings during the fifth and sixth centuries. With the spread of Christianity, religious architecture flourished; many churches and monasteries were erected. Early Christian churches were basilical in plan and had timber roofs. The oldest surviving church in Istanbul is the Basilica of St. John, located within the Studious Monastery. It is located in the southwest part of town, at Psammatia, near Yedikule. With its buautiful serpentine columns, richly carved marble architraves and opus sectile floor, the church is a fine example of early Christian art and architecture. The Basilica of Studious was converted into a mosque during the Ottoman period. It was well maintained until a fire in late nineteenth century destroyed its timber roof, also causing damage to the

Capital of the Marcian's column

marble columns and entablature. Today, the monument has no roof and its opus sectile floor is exposed to the elements.

Istanbul has suffered from fires throughout its long history. The second Hagia Sophia founded by Theodosius II was devastated by a fire which started during the Nike revolt in 532. The remains from this basilical structure were recovered during the excavations in the atrium of Hagia Sophia in 1930's. The floor of the second Hagia Sophia was found to be about 2.5 metres below the atrium level of the present Hagia Sophia. The surviving column bases of the second Hagia Sophia are preserved in situ. Huge architraves built of marble from the Proconnessian island, decorated with a frieze of lambs and a pediment block from the western gable give an idea about the beauty and the fine quality of the marble carving of the monument.

The three major monuments from the Justinianic period (532-565) Hagia Sophia, Hagia Eirene and Sergios and Bacchos were extraordinary projects of a remarkable age. The design of medieval churches was quite different from these earlier structures. Most of them were smaller in scale, due to the limited sources available for building programs. They usually had cross-in-square plans. The Lips Monastery Churches (Fenari İsa), Pantocrator (Zeyrek Camii), Churches of the Chora Monastery (Kariye Camii), Myraleion (Bodrum Camii), Pantepoptes (Eski Imaret Camii), Pammakaristos (Fethiye Camii), Gül Camii, Hagios Andreas (Koca Mustafa Paşa Camii), Vefa Kilise Camii, Theotokos Kyriotissa (Kalenderhane).

With its well preserved figural mosaics and frescos, Chora Monastery Church highlights the level of the decorative arts during the Medieval period. Though the largest of the medieval churches, the South Church of the Pantokrator Monastery, presently Zeyrek Camii, has only an opus sectile floor and some of its original marble revetment preserved in the interior. Not much survived from of its mosaic and other decoration due to sever earthquake damages and the Latin occupation of the city.

During the Latin occupation of Constantinople from 1204 until 1264, many of the valuable materials, icons, statues, capitals, marble revetments were removed from churches and the other monuments and taken to Europe, especially to Venice. With the recovery of the Paleologan dynasty, the damaged monuments were restored and the churches which had been converted to Latin ritual, were returned to Orthodox rite.

After the conquest of Constantinople by Mehmet II, most of the old churches were converted to become mosques; minbars vand mihrabs were added to their interior and minarets to their exteriors. Mosques connected to Mehmet II foundation like the Hagia Sophia and the south church of the Pantocrator also had imperial loggias reserved for the sultan.

The ancient city had several harbours on its southern and northern coasts. Neorion harbour (near Sirkeci of today) had

Theodosian Wall, Towers T17- T20

been in use since the Hellenistic period. The Theodosian and Sophianae harbours on the south coast were silted in time. Some old engravings from the Middle Ages and H. Schedel's drawing from the end of the fifteenth century, indicate two harbours on the Marmara coast: the Julian/Sophianae/Kontoskalion and the Eleutherios/Theodosius I harbours. The harbours are depicted as protected by sea walls; they have arched openings to let in the ships . Both of the harbours were silted and out of use during the Ottoman period. P. Gyllius who visited Istanbul during the sixteenth century noted that the old Kontoskalion harbour which was called Kadırga Limanı by the Turkish people, was already silted.

Instead of the ancient harbours on the southern coast of the city; Ottomans preferred the Golden Horn which is protected from the strong south wind that affects the sea considerably. Very little was known about the harbours until the recent rescue excavations for the subway provided the opportunity to carry out research into the silted Theodosian harbour. Excavations conducted at Yenikapı revealed very interesting and significant details about the history of the city. In the western part of the harbour, ruins of the harbour walls and timber posts to which the ships were tied were brought to light. More than twenty ship wrecks with loads of amphorae

Hagia Sophia

and other goods provided information about the nature of the Medieval seafaring of the city.

Very little has survived from the early palaces of Constantinople. During the construction of the Justice Palace in 1950's, remains of the Lausos and Antiochos Palaces were discovered. The design of the palaces in the Constantinian capital was closely related to the architectural tradition in Rome. These two palaces can be considered as representative of the many which have ben lost. Their proximity to the Mese can be interpreted as an indication of their importance.

The remains of the Great Palace of the Byzantine Emperors covers a wide area from the Hagia Sophia to the Marmara coast. The fire in 1912 removed the houses above the ruins and the first researches were made possible. Excavations conducted during 1930's at the Arasta of the Sultan Ahmet Complex uncovered a floor mosaic with mythological figures, hunting and daily life scenes. The location was identified as a one of the courtyards of the Palace. The mosaic was dated to the sixth century. Restoration of the mosaics took place between 1983-1994 as a joint venture between the Austrian Scientific Academy and the Turkish Ministry of Culture and Tourism. The deformed sections were removed from the ground, cleaned, stabilized and replaced in their original position by conservators. A new roof was built over the site, to protect it from the climatic conditions. The site has become the Mosaic Museum and is open to visitors.

During the restoration of the Tevkifhane, the old detention and later prison building dating from early twentieth century, some excavations were conducted in the courtyard and the surrounding area. The interesting finds from the ruins located to the north and west of the old prison provided new insight into the organization of the Great Palace. The finds from the digs are now exhibited within the Archaeological Museum of Istanbul. The in-situ remains, walls, decorated vaults, gates and other remains which are part the Great Palace await protection and presentation.

Romans supplied fresh water to the city from sources in the west and northern part of the town. Aqueducts and cisterns were constructed to bring water to the city and store it for times of war and siege. Aqueduct of Valens, also called Hadrianus Aqueduct with reference to Emperor Hadrian, is the earliest surviving water conveyance system in the town. It spanned the valley between two hills, starting from the fifth hill and reaching the fourth hill near the Theodosian Forum. Some claim that the stones from the walls of Chalcedon were used for its construction. The two storey structure has come through the centuries with several repairs. It continued to be used during the Ottoman period to transfer water from new sources. Pipes belonging to new conveyance systems, established by individuals were placed above it. The eastern part of the aqueduct collapsed during the earthquake of 1509. Today the Metropolitan Municipality is responsible for the maintenance of the monument. A major restoration of the structure was taken up in the 1990's. The monument suffers from the vibrations and the soot generated by the heavy traffic running under it.

There are quite a number of cisterns in the historic city. Some are called the open cisterns; they have large basins without a roof. The Aspar/Sultan Selim, Aetious/ Edirnekapı and Exi Marmara/ Seyitömer cisterns are of this kind; they could hold large quantities of water. Their thick and high walls have withstood time, but the conduits and the mechanical systems have disappeared. The open cisterns were abandoned during the Ottoman period. Some people used them for agricultural activity or built houses inside them. A small quarter with a masjid developed inside the Aspar cistern after the sixteenth century. In late twentieth century, the Municipality of Istanbul cleaned the accretions inside the cisterns. Today, the open cisterns are surrounded by densely built neighborhoods. Some are used as parks and playgrounds. Some temporary buildings, used for educational purposes are built within them, to make the most out of these vast structures. Considering their archaeological significance, these ancient monuments deserve to be treated more carefully, conserved and presented in a better way.

With their closely spaced columns and brick vaults, the underground cisterns are fascinating spaces to visit. Among them, the Basilica and Binbirdirek cisterns are the more impressive. Basilica Cistern which measures 138x64.6 meters in plan, was constructed in the sixth century. It is located very close to the Hagia Sophia and was in use throughout the Byzantine period. Ottomans preferred to use fresh water directly from the natural sources, so many of the Byzantine cisterns were not used and totally forgotten.

Parekklesion of Kariye Camii/ Monastery Church of Chora

The Basilica cistern was rediscovered in the nineteenth century and became a tourist attraction. There was still some water at its bottom and visitors used a boat to reach the far ends of its mystical interior. With the establishment of the Turkish Republic, the care of aqueducts and cisterns was handed over to the Metropolitan Municipality of Istanbul. During 1980's a comprehensive project was undertaken to clean the debris inside the cistern and restore the structure of this exquisite monument. During the implementation of the project, interesting details were brought to light. One of the discoveries was the frieze blocks with gigantic Medusa heads; these had been used as bases for some columns. Reuse columns and capitals from ancient monuments was common practice for Byzantines. The discovery was exciting because of the exceptional quality of the reused material. The restoration project included new lighting system and

Conservation and documentation work at one of the ship wrecks recovered at Yenikapı

walking platforms for the visitors. The cistern is now open to the public; occasionally artistic performances and cultural events are organized inside the cistern, taking advantage of its extraordinary atmosphere.

Though attributed to Philoxenes from the time of Constantine, the brick stamps date the construction of Binbirdirek cistern to the sixth century. The cistern is unique with its exceptionally tall columns composed of two shafts placed on top of each other. Its dark interior was used as a silk workshop during the ninetenth century. Today the property belongs to the General Directorate of Pious Foundations. After years of neglect, the interior was cleaned and restored by an investor. It is now open to the public; the interior is used for special meetings and art exhibits.

Several other cisterns have been discovered during excavations for new buildings. It is important to clean them and make accessible to the public, as part of the cultural heritage of the city. The cistern on Soğukçeşme Street near Hagia Sophia was one of the first to be restored and reused for tourism. The Touring and Automobile Club converted this small cistern close to Hagia Sophia and the Topkapı Palace into a restaurant. Recently, Nakilbent, Sultan Selim and Zeyrek cisterns have been restored, to be used for exhibits and other activities.

A detail from the mosaics of the Great Palace, exhibited at the Mosaic Museum

During the Byzantine rule, Genoese people were given the permit to settle to the north of the Golden Horn, in the area called Galata. This was a walled city; an independent settlement with its own administration. After the establishment of Ottoman rule in Constantinople, Genoese people continued to live there but several changes had to follow. The commercial center near the coast was reshaped. A bedesten was built in the center by Sultan Mehmet II. The great tower above the settlement was turned into a watchtower for fire and security. The settlement started to grow outside the walls. The embassies of European countries were established in the area to the north of the walls of Galata, in the area called Beyoğlu.

Ottoman Period

The transformation of Constantinople into the Ottoman capital took a long time to realize. Fatih Sultan Mehmet II, "the Conqueror", initiated projects to restore the city and improve the living conditions. He started the construction of the Topkapı Palace, Yedikule Castle, Fatih and Eyüp complexes, several commercial buildings, including three bedestens and a cannon foundry outside of the walls of Galata. These buildings served as some of the basic institutions needed for state administration, religious and educational needs, commercial activity and the defense functions.

To revive the city, an appeal was made to the inhabitants who had fled away during the siege to come back. New settlers were brought from the Balkans and Anatolia. Aksaray, and Karaman are two of the places from which people came in large groups to settle in the capital. The newly formed quarters took their names from the places which the settlers originated. Thus the name of the district Aksaray comes from Aksaray in central Anatolia, which people came and settled in the fifteenth century.

Complexes which usually included a mosque, a madrasa, a primary school and a bath were founded in different parts of the town by viziers and high ranking officers. These projects satisfied the religious, social and educational demands of the neighborhoods formed around them. Mahmut Paşa, İshak Paşa, Koca Mustafa Paşa, Murat Paşa are some of the viziers who have been active in reviving the city. New settlements also developed outside of the city walls; Eyüp, to the west of the historic town, Tophane to the north of Galata, Üsküdar and Kadıköy on the Asian side started to grow.

Fatih Complex, the religious and educational compound of Mehmet II was built on the fifth hill where the Holy Apostles Church and the tomb of Constantine stood before. The old church and the tomb had been neglected; the orthodox patriarch declined to stay there. So the site was used to build the complex of the new ruler. The project included a grand mosque, eight medreses, eight prep schools, a caravansaray, a guest house, a primary school, a hospital, a double bath and the tombs of the founder and his wife. The complex was organized like a great campus, with the mosque in the center and madrasas arranged symmetrically on the north and the south. The mosque which is considered as a step on the development of Ottoman mosques, had a big dome and a semi dome in the qibla direction.

The complex has come to our day with several changes. The earthquake of 1766 caused great damage to the mosque and the madrasas. The central dome collapsed. The scale of the structural damage necessitated the reconstruction of the mosque. The courtyard from the fifteenth century was preserved but the mosque the interior was rebuilt using a new scheme, composed of a central dome and four semidomes. The tombs of Fatih and his wife Gulbahar Hatun were also reconstructed after the earthquake of 1766.

Several losses and modifications have taken place in the Complex over the centuries. The primary school, hospital, the double bath, the caravansaray and kitchen have been lost in time. The recent earthquake of 1999 caused some cracks in the mosque, the guesthouse and the medreses. A project for the reinforcement of the endangered structures is going on.

During the sixteenth century, the city was embellished with several complexes founded by sultans and their family members, as well as by high officers of state. The imperial complexes offered several social, religious and educational service to their neighborhoods and also to the city. The model of the Fatih Complex was taken for the imperial foundations built in the sixteenth and seventeenth centuries. Their programs included a hospital, a guesthouse, a bath and the tombs in addition to an imperial mosque and educational buildings.

Complexes of Bayezıt II, Sultan Selim, Şehzade and Süleymaniye were the major projects of the sixteenth century. The care taken

Aqueduct of Valens, with madrasa of Gazanfer Ağa in the foreground

to design and execute them, their locations in the city are indicators of the care taken in dealing with urban topography. With their monumental compositions, the complexes aimed to exalt and eternalize the memory of their founders.

Bayezıt II Complex was raised in the center of the Historic Peninsula, close to the ancient Theodosian Forum. It is the second imperial complex founded by the Ottomans in the new capital. This part of the town acquired the name Bayezıt, after the establishment of the complex. The complex covers a wide area; to its east there is the grand Bazaar, on its west there was the Theodosian Arch. During the construction of the complex, some earlier buildings must have been removed. P. Gyllius who visited Istanbul in the middle of the sixteenth

Interior of the cistern on Soğukçeşme Street

century mentions that he wanted to see the Column of Theodosius and learned that it was removed about 40 years ago during the construction of the Bayezıt bath.

According to its Arabic inscription, the mosque of the Bayezıt Complex was built between the years 1501-1505. Starting about mid-fifteenth century, it became the tradition for Ottoman imperial mosques to have spacious courtyards surrounded with domed arcades. The mosque of Bayezıt has a beautiful courtyard with three monumental gates and arcades decorated with coloured marbles. The structural design of the mosque was influenced by Hagia Sophia; it has a central dome flanked by two semidomes, but much reduced in scale. The mosque followed the tradition of early Ottoman period, with guestrooms attached to the mosque. Two tall minarets attached to the ends of the entrance wall add to the monumentality of the mosque.

There is also a caravansaray, a public kitchen, a primary school, a medrese, a double bath and the tomb of the sultan. The imaret, caravansaray and the primary school constitute a group close to the mosque. The

116   General view of Galata

other buildings are detached from the mosque. The geometric site planning of the Fatih Complex could not be achieved here, due to the existing buildings in the area.

The mosque and the other members of the complex suffered from the 1509 earthquake which caused considerable damage to Istanbul's monuments. The main dome of the mosque was damaged. To stabilize the structure, the supporting arches and piers were reinforced. The earthquake of 1766 caused further damages to the mosque.

It is important that the complex has retained its integrity, with most of its members still intact. The caravansaray and public kitchen serve as part of the Bayezıt public library. The public kitchen is important as the earliest surviving example of this building type in Istanbul. Its functional units, like the kitchen, the refectory, cellars, bakery are organized around an arcaded courtyard. It sets a fine example for the Ottoman public kitchen; in fact, it has been taken as a model by architect Sinan for his design of Haseki and other public kitchens.

The primary school is a small building which lies to the southeast of the mosque. It consists of two parts. The first part of the building is a domed iwan; a roofed space but open to the courtyard. This part was like a porch to keep the children warm in winter.

The medrese of the complex is to the west of the mosque, detached from the other buildings. It has a classroom and cells organized around an arcaded courtyard in the form of a U; a typology which was very popular in Ottoman architecture. Bayezıt Medrese is a fine example of this type with its good proportions and elegant details. The medrese was transformed into a public library in the twentieth century. Recently, it has been converted into a museum for the art of calligraphy.

The double bath is a monumental building located to the southwest of the medrese, on one of the main streets of the city. When the level of the street was lowered during the road widening operations in 1950's, the foundations of the bath were exposed, revealing some re-used marble blocks from the Arch of Theodosius. The double bath has monumental dressing halls and beautifully decorated interior spaces; with almost symmetrically organized sections for men and women. Recently, it has been restored by Istanbul University to be used as a planetarium and a museum of astronomy.

During the Byzantine period, the buzzing commercial center of Constantinople was located on the northern hillside of the Historic Peninsula. It stretched from the forums of Theodosius and Constantine to the coast, which was used as the landing place for the goods entering the city by way of sea. Being in close relation with the harbour, the area continued its use for the commercial activity through the Ottoman period. Several shops, bedestens, inns, mosques, medreses, schools, baths were built to serve the needs of the tradesmen and the citizens. The names of the small ports reveal the type of activity which took place along the shore. Limon İskelesi (the port for lemons), Hatap İskelesi (the port for timber), etc. The old commercial center is still active and thriving with similar activities. The Egyptian Bazaar (Mısır Çarşısı), Mahmutpaşa, Tahtakale districts, Grand Bazaar are the places where daily life continues within its colourful atmosphere.

Istanbul, Castle of Yedikule

Some of the important caravansarays, like the Kürkçü Han from the fifteenth century or the Büyük Valide Han from the seventeenth century have suffered from earthquakes, neglect, change of ownership, lack of maintenance and crouching of unsuitable functions. At present, the commercial center of the historic city is on the verge of a serious transformation. The Metropolitan Municipality of Istanbul is developing projects for the rehabilitation of the area. There are plans to remove the accretions and restore the historic fabric carefully; to revive the commercial part of town and integrate it with the other parts.

The political and economic support to architectural activity was at its highest during the sixteenth century. Under the leadership of Mimar Sinan (1538-1588) several important projects were launched. Haseki, Şehzade, Süleymaniye, Kara Ahmet Paşa, Mihrimah Sultan, Rüstem Paşa, Sokollu complexes can be cited as some of the building programs which contributed to the improvement of the quality of urban life, as well as having an impact on the general outlook of the Historic Peninsula. The panorama of the city became even more attractive and pleasing to the eye with the construction of the Şehzade and Süleymaniye complexes. Mimar Sinan's contribution to the emergence of Istanbul's image as the Ottoman capital was outstanding.

Besides his service as the designer of magnificient complexes, Mimar Sinan worked like a civil engineer constructing aqueducts and bridges. He brought drinking water to the city from the north with a long conveyance system including several aqueducts. He stabilized Hagia Sophia, designed some pavillions and baths in the Harem of the Topkapı Palace.

The grand vizierial palaces surrounding Suleymaniye added to the attraction of the city. Of the impressive vizierial palaces scattered around the city, only the Ibrahim Pasha Place on the Hippodrome survives, though reduced in size and altered. Due to its position on the Hippodrome, Ibrahim Paşa Palace had a special role. It was used like a tribune from which the ceremonies taking place on the public square were watched. Especially the circumcision feasts of the young princes were the occasions when large crowds gathered on the Hippodrome and the sultan and the princes watched the games, or processions from the loggia overlooking the square. The palace was used for other purposes in late Ottoman period. Today it is turned into the Museum of Turkish and Islamic Arts, housing a rich collection of carpets, ceramic ware and ethnographic material, after a major restoration during the 1980s.

Ottoman power started to decline in the seventeenth century; the economic situation was not strong enough to support an energetic building program. Sultan Ahmet Complex, initiated at the beginning of the century, was the leading project of the period. The complex covered a vast area to the east and south of the ancient Hippodrome. It comprised of a monumental mosque with an imperial pavillion, a medrese, the tomb of the founder, a darulkurra, a public kitchen, a hospital, a public bath, houses and several shops for rent. Due to the difficulty of finding a large proper vacant place in the town center, the land for the buildings of the complex was acquired mainly by expropriation; some of the palaces near the Hippodrome were pulled down.

The southern end of the Hippodrome, the Sphendone, was included within the construction grounds. This are was used to build the hospital and the public kitchen buildings of the complex. As a result, the Hippodrome became a much smaller public square.

Several changes took place in the buildings and the area surrounding the Complex in the nineteenth and twentieth centuries. The hospital was transformed into an arts and crafts school in late nineteenth century. The school is still active and has incorporated the kitchen, cellars and the bakery of the complex into its premises. Another major change at the end of the nineteenth century was the construction of two new buildings on northern façade of the public kitchen. The Ministry for Mining and Forestry and the Janissary Museum buildings were raised on the southern side of the

Süleymaniye from the Golden Horn

Hippodrome. The two buildings were united internally during the twentieth century to be used as a school of economics and commerce. After a fire in 1979, the two buildings were restored to house the Rectorate of Marmara University and its auditorium.

In the second half of the seventeenth century, the unfinished mosque of Safiye Sultan, a structure which was initiated at the end of the sixteenth century near the shore at Eminönü, was taken up and completed by queen mother Turhan Valide Sultan. The name of the place, Eminönü, comes from the customs office for the goods brought to the city by ships. The locality was important commercially and inhabited by Jews. The queen paid for the expropriation of the land for the mosque and the additional buildings. The mosque was called Yeni Cami, meaning the "New Mosque", a name which has come to our day. The imperial lodge of Turhan Valide Sultan, her tomb, a monumental fountain and sabil, a covered bazaar, called the Egyptian Bazaar due to the spices coming from Egypt make up the program of the second imperial building venture of the seventeenth century.

Originally, the outer courtyard of the mosque was surrounded by the ancient sea walls in the north . During the nineteenth century, the sea walls near the shore were demolished to build office buildings between the coast and the mosque. These were removed in the middle of the twentieth century, enabling the impressive Yeni Cami to be visible again. The area surrounding the mosque is one of the busiest squares of the city, still vibrant with life; the spice, coffee and fish markets keep attracting crowds to walk through its streets.

The restricted economy of the seventeenth century lead to a significant reduction in construction activity. Grand viziers and notables like Kuyucu Murat Paşa, Ekmekçioğlu Ahmet Paşa, Bayram Paşa, Köprülü Mehmet Pasha, Merzifonlu Kara Mustafa Paşa established small complexes comprising a madrasa, a primary school, the tomb of the founder and a fountain. Today the madrasas are used as research institutes attached to universities or cultural associations.

The first quarter of the eighteenth century was called the Tulip Era; a time famous for the interest in flowers, poetry and leisure in Istanbul. Sultan Ahmet III had a palace at Kağıthane, near the river called the "Sweet waters of Europe". The section of the river passing through the palace grounds was paved with marble; several cascades, pavillions were built to make the place look like a heaven on earth.

During the eighteenth century, rococo and baroque styles were introduced to Istanbul by way of imported goods and diplomatic relations. Several kiosks at Kağıthane, some pavililons at Topkapı Palace, the mosques of Nur-u Osmaniye, Laleli and Eyüp reflect the development of the baroque style in architecture.

The sultans and their family members supported the construction of several fountains in the city. The Ahmet III Fountain in front of the entrance to Topkapı Palace is the most elegant and impressive of the sabil-fountain compositions from the period. The streets and the most frequented open spaces of the town were embellished with several beautiful fountains. Among the most beautiful, the wide eaved and richly decorated fountains at Tophane, Azapkapı, Üsküdar, Küçüksu and Emirgan can be cited.

During the nineteenth century, styles which were in fashion in Europe found their way into the Ottoman capital. In addition to European architects working for the sultan, some Ottoman citizens trained as architects in Europe introduced and adapted the current styles to Istanbul. Balyan family is famous for its members who have been court architects. They were responsible for the design and execution of several palaces and administrative buildings in Istanbul during the nineteenth century. As part of the westernization of Ottoman administration, several civil and military schools, barracks, stations, hospitals, offices, museums, ministries were raised in the city, transforming its image. Some of the travellers visiting Istanbul during the reign of Mahmut II have taken

Ibrahim Pasha Palace on the Hippodrome

Istanbul, Sultan Ahmet Mosque

notice of this rapid change and expressed their sorrow for the loss of the city's character.

After the earthquake of 1894, Raimondo D'Aronco, an Italian architect from Udine was invited by Sultan Abdülhamid II to work in Istanbul. He became the palace architect and is well known for his Art Nouveau designs in Yıldız Palace and on the Bosphorus. He also contributed to the restoration of some important monuments like the Mihrimah Sultan Mosque at Edirnekapı.

The Ministry of Agriculture, Forestry and Mining (now the Rectorate of the Marmara University), Janissary Museum, Imperial Medical School (Haydar Paşa Medical School, in collaboration with A. Vallaury), are some of the projects which show his involvement in Ottoman architecture. It was a time when revivalism was in the air. Architect Vedat Tek and Mimar Kemalettin Bey were the prominent local figures of the time, leading the style named "The First National

126 | Istanbul, Yeni Cami

Movement". Architect Kemalettin Bey designed the new housing complex which was raised on the site of the destroyed district of Laleli after the big fire of 1918. The Harikzedegan Apartments (1919-1922) project is known to be the first housing complex designed in the Historic Peninsula. It is now transformed into a hotel. Architect Vedat Tek is another significant figure of the First National Movement. Some of his buildings located in the Historic Peninsula. Like the Central Post Office, Hobyar Mescid, State Registers (Tapu Kadastro) and the Fourth Vakıf Han are considered to be landmarks from early twentieth century.

Towards the end of the nineteenth century, suburbs expanded in several directions; Göztepe and Feneryolu in the east, Bakırköy and Yeşilköy on the west, the Bosphorus villages to the north and the Prince's islands in the south were important with their timber residential architecture. Revival styles were in fashion. Several important summer houses in Art Nouveau

style attract the eye with their refined designs along the coast of the Bosphorus, at Bakırköy, Yeşilköy, Göztepe or the Prince's islands.

After a fire in the second half of the nineteenth century, Galata expanded outside of its walls, in several directions. Beyoğlu and Pangaltı districts developed with multi-storey housing. These areas were inhabited mainly by the Christian population of the city. Rue de Pera, today's İstiklal

Restored dome in the Imperial Pavillion of Yeni Cami

Caddesi, extended from Galata to Taksim; was further linked to Harbiye and Şişli where a new life style was starting. Many families living formerly in the Historic Peninsula left their private houses with gardens and moved to Nişantaşı, Teşvikiye and Şişli. This became the fashion for the Ottoman society who preferred to live in the European way. With the expansion of new districts, Taksim, Gümüşsuyu, Taşkışla, Maçka military barracks which were located outside of the settled areas of the city became surrounded with new neighborhoods from the late nineteenth and early twentieth centuries.

The Republican Period

With the fall of the Ottoman Empire, Ankara became the new capital of the Turkish Republic and the center of state affairs. Although Istanbul lost its priority in officially, it sustained its importance as the cultural, economic and industrial center of the country. The transition from the Ottoman to the Republican Period was followed by a conscious change in the legal and administrative system which had its effects in the outlook on architecture. The newly established state wanted to be part of the new idioms rather than sticking to the outdated revival styles. A new direction in architectural design was introduced to the new capital by the architects invited from Europe.

Some prominent architects continued their activities in Istanbul and designed important buildings in the Historic Peninsula. Among these the Faculty of Arts and Letters by Sedat Hakkı Eldem and Emin Onat (1944), Istanbul Publicity Center by Günay Çilingiroğlu and Muhlis Tunca (1969), the Social Security Buildings at Zeyrek by S.H. Eldem (1963) are worth mentioning.

Istanbul as World Heritage

In Istanbul, valuable vestiges of Roman, Byzantine and Ottoman periods; the Hippodrome, the Column of Constantine, ruins of the Great Palace, Theodosian Walls, underground cisterns, imperial churches and mosques, palaces, madrasas, caravansarays present a wide variety of archaeological and architectural repertoire. The grandeur of Byzantine Empire is best expressed in its capital with elegant, exquisite monuments. Several important Ottoman monuments, dating from the last five hundred years, also enrich the city; some continue to live with their original functions, some are adapted to serve as museums or other cultural institutions.

In contrast to the regular maintenance of the monumental heritage, the civil architecture of Istanbul is not so well protected due to several catastrophies. The fire of Hoca Paşa in 1865 caused great damage to the area around Sirkeci and Divanyolu. Widening the main streets like Alemdar and Divanyolu as a measure to facilitate movement of traffic resulted in further damage to the surviving buildings in the region. 1894 earthquake damaged masonry structures; several collapsed and had to be rebuilt. The great fires of Ishak Paşa (1912), Fatih, and Vefa devastated large parts of the city. Following the fires, the districts were not built according to the old street pattern but a grid-iron scheme was adopted. The reconstruction of the city according to a new layout, with different materials and scale had great impact on the loss of the surviving urban fabric.

By the middle of the twentieth century, there were attempts to facilitate traffic. In the early 1950's , during the construction of the Vatan and Millet boulevards, narrow streets were widened, the urban fabric was cut through without much care to preserve the historic city. Some monuments were moved or transferred to other locations. The new building regulation permitting the construction of high blocks on the new avenues introduced a new urban scale to the Historic Peninsula. This change aroused concern for the historic city and its surviving elements. Architects were critical about the drastic changes and tried to find the means to protect the surviving members of the traditional architecture.

The efforts to protect the urban fabric of the old city gained momentum in the second half of the twentieth century. At that time, the law for protection of cultural heritage permitted only the designation of individual houses. Historic houses had to have some special features like a monumental façade or a richly decorated interior, in order to be eligible for designation. It was not possible to designate groups of buildings, or streetscapes until 1973.

In 1973, a new law, which enabled the designation of urban sites was passed. Thus, it was possible for the Protection Board in Istanbul to designate Süleymaniye and Zeyrek districts, which were noted for their timber houses, as conservation areas.

In 1984, during the preparation of the nomination file for Istanbul, only the sites under legal protection, the Archaeological

Istanbul, World Heritage sign at Zeyrek

Park, Land Walls, Süleymaniye and Zeyrek districts were considered. Other historic areas, like the commercial center of town, including the Grand Bazaar and urban quarters like Fener-Balat districts were not included.

ICOMOS experts regarded the selected areas as the most prestigious of the historic city and representative of its past. Their report summarized the risks Istanbul was facing at the time. In 1984, the population of Istanbul was only two and a half million in comparison to the 12 millions of today. The report underlined the pressures emanating from traffic and urban growth.

Four separately protected sites,

1) The Archaeological Park,
2) The Süleymaniye quarter,
3) The Zeyrek quarter and
4) The zone of the ramparts,

were combined under the title "Historic Areas of Istanbul". World Heritage Committte adopted the proposal in December 1985 and the Historic Areas of Istanbul were included on the World Heritage List as number 356, on the basis of criteria i, ii, iii and iv.

i) The proposed cultural property includes unique monuments and masterpieces of universal architecture, such as Sophia which was built by Anthemios of Tralles and Isidoros of Milet in 532-5337 and the Süleymaniye mosque, a masterpiece of Sinan architecture.

ii) Throughout history, the monuments in the city center have exerted considerable influence on the development of architecture, monumental arts and the organization of space, both in Europe and in Asia. Thus, the 6,650 meter terrestrial wall of Theodosius II with its second line of defences, created in 447, was one of the leading references for military architecture even before St. Sophia's became a model for an entire family of churches and later mosques and before the mosaics of the palaces and churches of Constantinople influenced the Eastern and Western Christian art.

iii) Istanbul bears unique testimony to the Byzantine and Ottoman civilizations.

iv) The Palace of Topkapı and the Süleymaniye mosque with its annexes (Caravanserail, madrasa, medical school, library, hamam, hospice, cemetery, etc.) provide the best examples of

131

ensembles of palaces and religious complexes of the Ottoman period.

Archaeological Park

Until recently, it was customary to start the history of Istanbul with Byzantion and claim that the city has cultural levels which go back 2,700 years. Recently rescue archaeology at Yenikapı, within the ancient harbour of Theodosius, revealed human existence dating back to prehistoric times. This revolutionary discovery provided a much earlier date for human existence at the Historic Peninsula, yet the level at which the physical remains were found were under the sea level. So the chronology of human settlement needs to be analyzed in relation to the tectonic movements in the area.

The better known history of the city starts with Byzantion, which was inhabited by colonists from Greece and then by the Romans and Ottomans. Due to the later settlements over the same site, there are areas and levels which have not been fully researched. Urban planner Mr. Henri Prost was invited by the Municipality in 1930's to prepare a regulatory plan for Istanbul. The planner appreciated the archaeological potential of the city and designated the eastern end of the Historic Peninsula as an Archaeological Park. The Park stretched from the Bosphorus in the east to the Basilica Cistern and the Hippodrome in the west, from the Golden Horn in the north to the Marmara Sea in the south. The plan foresaw archaeological research to reveal the ancient remnants of the city and proposed to preserve and present them to the public. Topkapı Palace, the Great Palace of the Emperors, Sultan Ahmet Complex, Ibrahim Paşa Palace, Basilica Cistern and Binbirdirek are among the most important monuments and complexes within this vast area. They are mainly owned by the State and maintained with public funds. The privately owned plots would be expropriated and removed in order to present the archaeological finds within an archaeological park. Although foreseen in the urban plan, due to lack of funds, the Archaeological Park never came to life.

The remains of the Great Palace are dispersed over a wide area and threatened by tourism development. The recent extension of the Four Season's Hotel is a problem which was discussed by experts and the public. It is essential to take the initiative to unite the plots on which the remains are located and establish the measures for integrated protection and presentation of the whole. Similarly, there are problems related to the management of Topkapı Palace. The Palace grounds contained within the walls (Sur-u Sultani and Sea Walls) has been divided and acquired among several public institutions. This situation makes it hard to manage, protect and present the Palace to the public.

Within the Archaeological Park, there are several monuments and ancient ruins. From these, the major ones are selected and presented below.

Hagia Sophia

After becoming the capital of the Eastern Roman Empire, Constantinople was embellished with Christian monuments. The early churches have been changed or modified in time due to fires and reconstructions. The Hagia Sophia which is standing today is the third one erected on the same spot. Excavations conducted in 1930s, within the atrium of Hagia Sophia revealed the portico of the second Hagia Sophia dating from 415.

According to the walls and the column bases preserved in situ, the second Hagia Sophia was a five nave basilica. This church suffered from the fire initiated during the Nika revolt in 532. Emperor Justinian delegated the design to two outstanding technicians of the period: Anthemios from Tralles and Isidoros from Miletus. Justinian's desire was to erect a monument which would be a monument used for coronations. Construction which started in 532 proceeded quickly and the church covered by a magnificent dome and two semidomes was inaugurated in 537. The nave covered was surrounded by galleries on its three sides. Mosaics with gold and silver tesserae, purple and grey, green, white and honey colored marbles added to the grandeur of the interior. The church was part of larger complex containing the patriarchate, baptisterium and the treasury-Skeuphylakion.

Twenty years after its construction, in 557, the large dome of Hagia Sophia, spanning more than 33 meters, was damaged by an earthquake. It collapsed in 558, destroying the altar, ciborium and the ambon. During the restorations conducted by Isidoros the Younger, the form and height of the dome was changed. Instead of the earlier saucer dome, a hemispherical dome was erected on top of the pendentives. The reopening of the church took place in 563. During the Iconoclastic period, all the figural decoration in the church was removed; as

Istanbul, Hagia Sophia, mosaic over the Imperial door

a result of which all the existing figural mosaics in Hagia Sophia are from the medieval period.

The structure has been exposed to severe tremors throughout its long history. The earthquake in 869 caused some damages. The earthquake of 989 destroyed the western arch supporting the dome as a result of which the semidome in that direction had to be renewed. The repair after this serious damage was carried out by the Armenian architect Trdat. He reconstructed the western semidome and fifteen ribs of the main dome.

The earthquake in 1343 caused new cracks in the structure; the eastern semidome and one third of the eastern part of the main dome collapsed in 1346. The restoration of Hagia Sophia after this catastrophe was completed in 1353. The scar remaining from this damage can be seen on the eastern elevation of the monument.

Following the Ottoman conquest, Hagia Sophia was converted into a mosque. As the nearest mosque to Topkapı Palace, it had the status of an imperial mosque. Mehmet II allocated large sums of money for the repairs of Hagia Sophia, enabling it to be well maintained through the centuries. A medrese and a minaret were constructed to make it a mosque and initiate a complex. Later more minarets were added. This grand monument was Ottomanized further by additional inner fittings and annexes by the donations of the succeeding sultans. Through the centuries, the interior has been enriched with new furniture, calligraphy panels, mihrabs, mahfils, objects brought from ancient ruins.

In 1573 with the permission acquired from Selim II, Mimar Sinan cleared away the houses crouching on Hagia Sophia's walls and repaired the south façade of the monument. When Selim II died in 1576, he was buried to the south of Hagia Sophia; his monumental tomb was designed by Architect Sinan. Later the tombs of Murat III and Mehmet III were also constructed in the garden of Hagia Sophia, which resulted in the creation of a densely built area to the south of the monument.

The Baptistry of the Hagia Sophia was located to the south of the church and had its entrance from the north side. It is octagonal in plan and covered by a dome. After the conversion of the church into a mosque, it stopped being used, becoming a storage place for candles. In 1639 , it was used to bury Sultan Mustafa I, thus became included to the group of imperial tombs in the garden of Hagia Sophia. The marble basin belonging to the original building was probably removed to bury the sultan. The font is preserved and stands in the porch of the monument preserved. Later the baptisterium was used to bury Sultan Ibrahim I also. The interior was probebly painted in the Ottoman fashion during the conversion. Very little survives from the original mosaic decoration of the building.

Mahmut I added an ablution fountain, a primary school, a library and a public kitchen to the Hagia Sophia Complex. With its wide eaved roof and dome, the ablution fountain is a richly decorated and monumental piece of architecture, embellishing the courtyard. The library was squeezed between two buttresses on the south façade of the monument. It has a reading room accessible from the interior of the Hagia Sophia, and a stack on the south façade. The addition of a public kitchen to the complex was important; as all the major

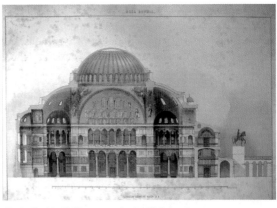

Hagia Sophia, E-W cross-section by W. Salzenberg

imperial establishments in Istanbul had kitchens to serve meals to the staff, students and the poor people.

The earthquake of 1766 did no major damage to Hagia Sophia, yet due to its deteriorated condition, the monument underwent a major restoration between 1847-1849 by the order of Sultan Abdülmecit. The works were directed by Fossati brothers from Italy. During this major operation, the mosaics were revealed by removing the plaster over them. They were documented, the exterior of the monument was plastered and painted with red and white stripes to simulate an alternating wall construction. A sultan's lodge was added to the end of the north gallery. Other buildings added during this repair are the medrese and the muvakkithane (clock room for setting the prayer times).

The earthquake of 1894 caused some damages in Hagia Sophia and a restoration campaign was started by the Ministry of Pious Foundations/ Waqf adinistration. After the establishment of the Turkish Republic, there was an intention to convert this religious edifice into a museum. In 1935 by means of a special law, Hagia Sophia became a museum. This made it possible to have researches under the plasters to reveal figural mosaics and present them to the public. At present the monument is protected by the Ministry of Culture and Tourism. There are three departments responsible for the administration, conservation and restoration of the museum. The museum directorate is in charge of the administration of the museum, the conservation laboratory is responsible for conducting monitoring and conservation operations, the Survey and Monuments Directorate contracts firms for maintenance works and supervises them.

The restoration of the dome mosaics which started with the support of the UNESCO in early 1990's, continued with funding from World Monuments Fund and the Ministry of Culture and Tourism. A 55 m high scaffolding was designed specially for the restoration of the dome mosaics. The scaffolding, which covered only one quarter of the floor area was rotated around the central area, until all of the dome mosaics were examined, recorded and restored.

The study and monitoring of the structure of Hagia Sophia is important because of earthquakes which might cause serious damages in the future. A project was started in 1988 to monitor the structure of Hagia Sophia by the Bosphorus and Princeton Universities. Turkish Ministry of Culture and Tourism established a scientific committee which has both national and international members to discuss and supervise the conservation works on the structure.

Hagia Irene

Hagia Irene is one of the major churches founded by Emperor Justinian in the sixth century. Though repaired and modified several times due to earthquakes, it still preserves some of its original features like its atrium, three naved structure and synthronon. After the earthquake in 740, the top of its gallery and decoration was renewed. During the Ottoman period, it was included within the Topkapı Palace grounds, which detached it from the public. It stopped functioning as a religious building but was used as a repository of arms. In the ninetenth century, the first Ottoman museum was established

Hagia Irene, main dome and the supporting arches

here. With the foundation of a military museum at Harbiye, the objects were moved there and Hagia Eirene was ready to be used for other cultural purposes.

After restoration works conducted between 1973-74, the monument started to be used for musical performances, exhibits and similar activities. With its beautiful acoustics and interior, it is an attractive place for concerts.

During a recent alteration, the arcades around the atrium were reorganized to house the mosaics which had been recovered in rescue digs at different locations in the city. The presentation and reuse of this important monument needs to be reconsidered. It is important to have Hagia Irene open to the public but the type of activities taking place in it should not be contradictory to its significance and meaning. The vulnerability of Hagia Eirene is being assessed within the ISMEP (Istanbul Seismic Risk Mitigation and Emergency Preparedness) Project which is supported by the World Bank.

TOPKAPI PALACE

After the Conquest of Istanbul, the capital of the Ottoman State was moved to Istanbul and several important projects were initiated. One of the priorities was to rehabilitate the city which had been deserted and neglected during the siege. The construction of the Fatih Complex, Topkapı Palace and commercial buildings are among the most significant projects related to the establishment of religious, social, educational, administrative and commercial institutions. Some of the decisions taken to repair and found important centers have been influential in the building of a good looking and impressive capital.

Topkapı Palace is one of the rare examples of a palace surviving from the fifteenth century. It has a great impact on the skyline of the city. To place the administrative center of the Empire over the old acropolis of Byzantion was an important decision which has affected the structure and the silhouette of the city over the centuries. A huge area covering 700,000 square meters was allocated to the palace grounds. The ruins of Hellenistic, Roman and Byzantine periods were incorporated in its grounds. The natural lines of the hill were modified by terraces supported on retaining walls and substructures.

With centuries of use and building, renovations, Topkapı Palace is an architectural treasure, incorporating structures both from the early days of its foundation and the last days of its use as the abode of the Ottoman sultan. It was the decision of Sultan Mahmut II to desert Topkapı Palace and move to live at the palaces on the Bosphorus. The Palace became a museum in the twentieth century, after the establishment of the Turkish Republic. All the interesting objects the sultans used and collected: Books, antiques and art objects are kept and exhibited within the Topkapı Palace Museum. Interiors with rich Baroque decoration from late eighteenth century can be found in the Harem premises.

The area on which the Palace is founded was already surrounded by the Byzantine fortifications from the north and south. The western wall of Mehmet II's Palace are called Sur-u Sultani (The Imperial Wall). It starts from Ahırkapı on the Marmara coast and rises uphill nearing a point very close to Hagia Sophia. This is also the highest point of the first hill. From here the wall advances towards the north, going down towards the Golden Horn and terminating at a point called Demir Kapı (the Iron Gate). The construction of this huge wall took many years. Starting in 1459, it continued during Mehmet II's lifetime and was completed after his death in 1481. The wall is three meters thick and reinforced with 28 towers most of which are square in plan. Towers have two floors and a roof level. A wall walk runs above the lower part of the walls at the first floor level of the towers. The platform levels of the towers were designed for shooting out with cannons.

The main entrance to the Palace grounds is called the Bab-ı Hümayun/The Imperial Gate and is located at the highest point of the first hill. Originally, the imperial gate had an upper floor, which is visible in drawings from the nineteenth century. During a restoration in late nineteenth century, the upper floor was removed and the building was finished with a corbelled cornice. Bab-ı Hümayun is the most monumental of the entrances to the Topkapı Palace grounds; there are several smaller gates, smaller in scale and modest in design. Some were named according to their location or special features. The changes in the nineteenth and twentieth centuries resulted in the loss of some of the walls and the management of Topkapı Palace is divided among several institutions. The northern end of the Imperial Wall was demolished during the construction of the railroad in the second half of the nineteenth century. Military institutions were established within the northern part of the outer gardens. At the moment the Topkapı Palace Museum occupies only the core of the original Palace, but there are attempts to unite the grounds of the earliar Palace under one administration.

The Palace developed around three inner courts. The first courtyard was open to the public; the level of privacy ascended as one moved towards the inner parts of the Palace. Around the first courtyard several workshops, the office of the mayor of the city, the dormitories of the palace guards, hospital of the palace, storage areas for wood and food, boat keeping places, farming areas were arranged. Hagia Eirene is also within this courtyard. The area to the north of the courtyard was called Gülhane, the Rose Garden. In 1910, Sultan Reşat (r. 1908-1918) donated this part of the Palace grounds to the citizens of Istanbul, making it a public park. A new gate was opened for the purpose of providing access to the northern part of the palace grounds. This gate is still in use, providing access to the public park, the Archaeological Museum and the Çinili Kiosk.

Çinili Kiosk was one of the places for the enjoyment of the Sultan. It was built in 1472 near the javelin playing grounds. With its special interior design comprising four iwans surrounding a central hall covered by a high dome, it recalls the contemporary monumental buildings of Semerkand. Its tile decoration also reflects eastern influences. During the fourteenth and fifteenth centuries several craftsmen came or were invited from Iran and central Asia. The original porch which had timber columns, like its contemporaries in Uzbekistan, suffered from a fire in the eighteenth century and was restored in stone.

This unique monument was turned into a museum in 1880 and serves as the Tile Museum since 1981. There is an extensive collection of interesting architectural elements made of tiles, like mihrabs and inscriptions collected from medieval and Ottoman monuments. The ceramic utensils, oil lamp collections give an idea about the history of the glazed ceramic production in Turkey. The museum was restored in 2004-05 and opened again with an improved presentation.

Topkapı Palace had several small summer pavillions perched on the sea walls or built along the coast, for the sultan or his family, affording a beautiful view over the Bosphorus and the Golden Horn. Some of the kiosks were used for certain ceremonies. In some engravings from the nineteenth century, Yalı

Istanbul, Topkapı Palace, Çinili Kiosk

kioks is depicted as the building used for ceremonies. The sultan and his retinue watched the Ottoman ships leave the harbour at Yalı Kiosk. A similar ceremony took place when the fleet entered the Golden Horn on its return from sailing in the far seas. Unfortunately, the coastal kiosks have not been well preserved. During the construction of the railroad in late 19th century, they were removed. Yalı Kiosk was completely destroyed; only the substructure of the Incili Kiosk and Sepetçiler kiosks remained. The railroad damaged the connection of the coastal kiosks with Palace grounds. Sepetçiler kiosk was built in 1643, over the sea walls. It had a veranda and hall covered with a dome. It is claimed that this kiosk was used by the ladies of the harem to watch the Ottoman fleet sail out from the Golden Horn. The kiosk was in a ruined state until 1980s. It was restored by the government in early 1990s and is now used for symposia and international press meetings.

Alay Kiosk, which is situated over a tower located on the western Walls of Topkapı Palace, had an important role. It was the loggia from which the sultan watched the parade of Istanbul's guilds. The first kiosk,

which was probably made of timber, was constructed during the reign of Murat III (1574-1595). Evliya Çelebi relates in detail how the architects proceeded in the parade past this kiosk. The present Alay Kiosk was built in 1819, during the reign of Mahmud II. It is located across the Gate to the High Port, over a turn the wall makes towards the north. As one walks along the walls of the Palace, its monumental dome attracts the attention. It is accessible from Gülhane Park and is approached by a ramp. Its spacious halls and rooms are used by the Ministry of Culture and Tourism.

Two important building groups have been added to the first courtyard of the Palace in the eighteenth and nitneeenth centuries. The first is the Royal Mint buildings, which started to develop in the area to the west of Hagia Eirene, starting from first half of the eighteenth century. The existing mint buildings are from the nineteenth century. The Mint continued to function at its historic premises until the second half of the twentieth century. After 1980s, it moved to new premises and the historic buildings were handed over to the Ministry of Culture.

The second group of buildings are the museums which were added in late nineteenth century. The Archaeological Museum was designed and built between 1891-1907 by A. Vallaury to house the finds from excavations. The Museum of Ancient Oriental Civilizations which is to the north of

General view of Topkapı Palace from the north, with Sepetçiler Kiosk on the Golden Ho

the Archaeological Museum, was built as an art school and later transformed into a museum.

The entrance to the second courtyard of Topkapı Palace is through a monumental gateway flanked by two octagonal towers. Only the sultan could pass through this gate on horseback. Others had to walk in. Administrative and service buildings like Divanhane, the council of ministers, outer treasury and the kitchens surround the second courtyard. The council room, which consists of two domed rooms, is on the north side. The sultan occasionaly participated in the meetings of the ministers. He could listen to the discussions, secretly, behind the latticework of a window from Adalet Kulesi, the tower attached to the council room. This tower was lower in the fifteenth century design, as can be seen from the miniature of Matrakçı Nasuh from sixteenth century and the engraving of Melling from the beginning of the nineteenth century. The tower symbolized the justice of the sultan. It was heightened and its top was remodelled in the current revival style during the nineteenth century.

The kitchen, with its cellars and dormitories of the cooks lie on the southern part of the courtyard. The kitchens from the fifteenth century were remodelled by Mimar Sinan after a fire in 1574. According to historic documents from 1478, fourtysix men worked in the kitchen and bakery; consisting of twentyfour cooks, nine bakers and thirteen tasters.

The entrance to the third court is called Bab-üs Saade, the Gate of Felicity. The coronation ceremonies took place in front of this gate. The gate underwent a major restoration in 1774, under the reign of Abdulhamid I; the central part of the arcade on the eastern part of the courtyard was cut and a baroque canopy was inserted in the middle.

The third courtyard, Enderun was the private domain of the sultan. Across the entrance, there is the Reception Hall, where the sultans received their foreign guests. It consists of a rectangular reception hall, surrounded by high arcades.

The interior and the exterior of the hall are lavishly decorated with coloured marbles, glazed tiles and gilding. Some old engravings show the sultan sitting on the throne and receiving envoys. The kiosk preserves much of its original features though renovated after a fire in the nineteenth century.

The third courtyard is built over a sloping terrain. The ground is inclined towards the east. The Reception Room stands at the highest point of the courtyard and is connected to the surrounding area with stairs. The kiosk of Fatih is located at the southeast corner of the courtyard. On the north side of the courtyard, there is the mosque for the guards. The Palace school where the guards at the service of the sultan were trained was also in this courtyard.

The fifteenth century layout of the Palace was modified in the course of later centuries. One of these was the transformation of the Has Oda, the Sultan's Room, to Hırka-i Saadet Dairesi, the Suite for the Holy Relics of Islam in the sixteenth century, after the Conquest of Egypt by Sultan Selim I. Another important change was the addition of a library to the east of the Reception Hall by Ahmet III in the eighteenth century.

Alay Kiosk on the Sur-u Sultani/ walls surrounding the Topkapı Palace from the wes

Until the seventeenth century, the area to the east of the third courtyard was like the outer gardens of the Palace. This part of the Palace developed in the seventeenth century. Several beautifully decorated pavillions, the Iftariye, Revan and Bagdad kiosks were built for the sultan to rest, read and enjoy the Golden Horn and the Bosphorus. The Kiosk of Kara Mustafa Pasha which also dates from the seventeenth century is also within this part of the Palace. It is one of the oldest timber buildings in the Palace. During the Tulip Period, this part of the Palace was used for night entertainments, with tortoises carrying candles.

Starting with Mahmud II, the sultans moved to the palaces on the Bosphorus, leaving Topkapı Palace to guards and elderly women. Yet, the archive, library and collections were kept as part of the history of the place. Sultans visited the Palace occasionally, for some ceremonies or events. Sultan Abdülaziz asked architect Sarkis Balyan to design a kiosk for him. Mecidiye Kiosk which is the last kiosk built within the Topkapı Palace overlooks the Bosphorus. A small mosque and guard house were associated with this project. At a spot to the east of Mecidiye Kiosk, there is the Column of Goths

Topkapı Palace, third courtyard

which was put up to celebrate the victory of the Romans over the Goths. The fifteen meters tall column has a beautiful capital with an eagle carved in low relief.

During the ninenteeth century, several important projects were realized in Istanbul. The construction of the Istanbul-Paris railroad is noteworthy for its impact on Topkapı Palace. The railroad was constructed but it stopped at the outskirts of the city, at Yedikule. To build a station in the center was almost impossible because, to reach Sirkeci, the railroad had to cut through the Palace gardens. Sultan Abdulaziz was convinced about the benefits of the railroad coming to the center of the city. So he gave permission to cut through the Topkapı Palace grounds. This resulted in the demolition of some pavillions belonging to the Palace, as well as damage to historic walls and towers.

Harem

Harem is the section of the Palace reserved for the vives, concubines, children of the sultan. There were also guards and maids working to carry out the services. Its entrance is from the second court, at a point to the north of the Council Hall. Another door opens into the third courtyard. Harem people lived within the rooms, apartments, pavillions and wards located in the northern part of the second and third courtyards.

There are doubts about the presence of a harem in the original design of the Topkapı Palace; the family of Mehmet II lived in the Old Palace at Bayezıt, near the Forum Tauri before the construction of Topkapı Palace. The separation of the family from the New Palace came to an end in the sixteenth century. During the reign of Sultan Suleyman the harem section started to develop. The construction of some pavillions at Topkapı Palace by Mimar Sinan and Davut Ağa are recorded in several documents from the sixteenth century.

The harem has a very complex structure; it has grown spontaneously over the centuries. Since it was attached to the north wall of the Palace, new development had to be towards the north, over retaining walls and substructures. The drop in the land towards the north afforded a beautiful view towards the Golden Horn and Galata. Harem continued its growth in the seventeenth and eighteenth centuries. The kiosk of Osman III is one of the most attractive designs from the eighteenth century. The kiosk has a jetty which projects over the high retaining wall separating the harem from

Topkapı Palace, court of the Black Eunuchs in the Harem

the Gülhane Park. Its interior is purely baroque in style, reflecting the influences from France.

Besides the many rooms for women and the long corridors, there are many special spaces like baths, private suites built for some sultans, the premises of the queen mother, the ward of the guards. The gardens of the harem were carefully guarded, not to let outsiders to trespass into the private grounds. The harem did not have a kitchen of its own, the meals were served from the kitchens in the second court.

Topkapı Palace was transformed into a museum in 1924, soon after the establishment of the Turkish Republic. This was the

starting point for the systematic study and documentation of its movable and immovable heritage. Architects Selma Emler and Mualla Eyüpoğlu Anhegger worked on the different sections of the Palace to restore and present the large complex as a museum. The mosque of the guards became the library for manuscripts. The kitchens, Fatih's pavillion, outer treasury were transformed into exhibition halls for the china, jewellery and the armory collections. The cellars became the archive for the documents related to the history of the Palace and several buildings founded by the sultans. The archive is very rich with its collection of documents related to the personal life of the imperial family and the other inhabitants of the Palace and the construction activity of the imperial family. It is worth noting that the construction books of Sultan Ahmet Complex are preserved in this archive, along with many other documents related to repairs and reconstructions of mosques, castles and bridges.

During the restorations, researches were conducted, to understand the evolution of the structures and their transformations. Some of the different phases of interventions are visible and reflect the changes in taste and style.

The harem was cleaned of the inappropriate additions made in late nineteenth century, by those left behind after Mahmud II and his family left Topkapı Palace to move to the palaces on the Bosphorus. At areas where the unity of the interior is at risk, the last period of decoration was preserved with only small sections to indicate the findings from the earlier phases. The harem was opened to the public after the lengthy restorations.

Interesting details were uncovered in the process of cleaning and restoration. The discovery of the original dome of the Veliaht Dairesi, the Pavillion of the crown prince was not visible because of the construction of a timber ceiling during the late nineteenth century. The original dome with its exquisite decoration on deer hide was revealed and restored. It is one the exceptional pieces of seventeenth century architecture.

The restoration and maintenance of the artifacts and architectural treasures of the Palace requires funds allocated regularly from the Ministry of Culture budget. The projects are developed and implemented by the Survey and Monuments Department of the Ministry of Culture and Tourism and the staff of the Conservation Laboratory. A management plan is on the way for the protection of this exceptional treasure. Topkapı Palace has been exposed to several earthquakes in its long history and restorations followed the cracks and collapses. Recently there is a project by the Ministry of Culture and Tourism to prepare for the earthquake expected in 30 years.

1.The SÜLEYMANİYE quarter

Süleymaniye quarter incorporates a good collection of timber houses which have not suffered from the fires in early twentieth century as well as very significant monuments and complexes. The site spans from Ragıp Pasha Avenue in the north to Shehzade Complex in the south and from Uzun Çarşı street/Macro Embolos in the east to Atatürk Boulevard in the west. Besides the extensive complex of Süleymaniye, the ancient aqueduct of Valens, Vefa Camii, a medieval church, the sixteenth century Shehzade Complex, Atıf Efendi Library from the eighteenth century, the Ottoman Ministry of War (now the Istanbul University Rectorate), the headquarters of Istanbul Muftu, Botanic Institute attached to Istanbul University are located within this district.

Süleymaniye Complex and the settlement around it has an important place within the Golden Horn silhouette of the Historic Peninsula. Süleymaniye Complex gave the district its name. It is a grand establishment reflecting the glory of the Ottoman Empire in the sixteenth century. Its program reflects the might and generousity of the imperial founder. The general layout of the complex follows the axiality of the Fatih Complex; the mosque is in a central position. It rises like a mountain over the top of the hill and catches the eye as one looks towards the Historic Peninsula from the north.

The land needed for the construction of the Complex was partly allocated from the Old Palace grounds. The rest was acquired by expropriation. Due to the sloping terrain towards the north and west, terraces were created by the construction of retaining walls. It took nearly nine years (1550-59) to build the complex which consists of a grand mosque, two tombs, a primary school, five madrasas, one medical college, a hospital, a caravansaray, a guesthouse, a refectory, a kitchen, a bakery, a Koran reading room, a bath and several shops. A spacious courtyard surrounds the mosque and its arcaded couryard on three sides. The tomb of the founder and his wife are placed to the qıbla side of the mosque, in the garden to the southeast. Madrasas are on the northeast and southwest sides of the mosque. The northwest side is reserved for three major buildings of the complex; the hospital, the refectory-kitchen and the tabhane/guesthouse. Due to the slope towards the west, all of the three buildings have basements.

The structural scheme of Süleymaniye mosque was inspired by Hagia Sophia, however, Mimar Sinan chose a more modest scale for his mosque design, probably due to the imminent earthquake risk. The dome of Süleymaniye is 24 meters in diameter, in contrast to the 33 meter wide dome of Hagia Sophia. Mimar Sinan contributed to the sixteenth century mosque design with many important, new details. He regarded Süleymaniye as the work of his mid-career. The three storeyed western gate of the courtyard is unique in Ottoman architecture. Marble, granite, porphyry columns were brought from different places of the Empire to embellish this grand monument. The best quality works of stone masons, tile workers and other craftsmen of the time were used in the creation of Süleymaniye.

For the first time in Ottoman architecture, the ablution fountains were placed on the side walls of the mosque. In the courtyard, a decorative fountain with jets of water from its ceiling was a novice. The treatment of the structural elements, especially the buttresses on the side elevations was very ingenious. They were nicely articulated; the combination of the rythmic two-storeyed arcade and its projecting roof was a novelty in the façade design of Ottoman mosques.

Mimar Sinan used references to ancient architecture in his major works, enriching his designs and giving them a depth of history. Octagonal plan was used very often for tombs in Ottoman architecture. In his design for the tomb of Sultan Süleyman, Mimar Sinan used an octagonal plan with inner

Süleymaniye Complex, first and second madrasas

and outer ambulatories, borrowing elements from Roman architecture.

The tomb of Roxelane, the dear wife of Süleyman the Magnificent is located very close to his but is quite modest in scale. The plan is octagonal on the outside, but sixteen sided inside. This typology is derived from Seljuk architecture; Mimar Sinan had several references to Seljuk architecture in his works. The interior of the tomb is richly decorated with

glazed tiles. The exterior is sober with regular ashlar masonry. The cylindical drum of the tomb is unique in Ottoman architecture, with verses from the Quran carved on it.

Madrasas

There are six madrasas within the Complex of Süleymaniye. The first four were the highest level universities of their time. They were called the first, second, third and fourth in Ottoman (Evvel, Sani, Salis and Rabi) . The first two madrasas are located on the southwest side of the mosque, on a land sloping towards the north. They are arranged symmetrically on two sides of a street. Today these two madrasas are used by the Ministry of Culture and Tourism as the manuscript library for the collections of the historic libraries of Istanbul. A team of conservators are employed for the care of the rare books in the library.

The third and fourth madrasas are on the northern side of the mosque, overlooking the Golden Horn. They are also symmetrical in layout, with their entrances located on

Tabhane/guesthouse of the Süleymaniye Complex

the Mimar Sinan Street. The tomb of Mimar Sinan is also located on this street. The madrasas do not have inscriptions; historic documents provide the date they started to function as 1558. The design of the northern twin madrasas is very special; their courtyards are not level but adapted to the terrain with steps. The classrooms are located at the highest point of the land. The courtyard has several terraces. One reaches the northern wing of the building by means of steps. The eastern and western arcades have sofas for the students to sit, read or contemplate. Under the northern wing of the third and fourth madrasas , there is a row of rooms dedicated to the accommodation of poor scholars. These rooms were later named Mülazımlar Medresesi, the Madrasa of Scholars, although the building did not function as a madrasa.

The fifth madrasa is the Darülhadith; a madrasa for the teaching of the sayings of the prophet Mohammad. This madrasa was the highest ranking madrasa in the Ottoman Empire, when it was built. It consists of a raised classroom and a row of cells arranged on a broken line. The madrasa was damaged seriously in the course of time; today it is difficult to trace some of the original features.

The sixth madrasa was for medical studies; it was the first medical school in Istanbul. It is located to the west of Sani madrasa, with its cells placed above the western end of Tiryaki Çarşısı, the bazaar of tobacco dealers. According to the foundation deed of Süleymaniye Complex, there were eight students in the medrese. This means that there were eight rooms for the students and other spaces for the staff and services. Medical college was converted to a hospital in the twentieth century. Today there are twelve rooms arranged in a line. The two rooms at the ends are rectangular in plan and covered with two domes. The others are square in plan. Within the present arrangement, there is not a large room which could be used for lectures. Probably, both the theoretical courses and practical exercises took place in the hospital building. Originally, there was probably a colonnade or an arcade with a timber roof along the southern side of the cells. Several changes took place; the arcade is no longer a semi-open space but walled in.

The single domed building attached to the eastern wall of the tomb garden is the Darülkurra, the building for teaching the different styles of Quran reading. In a map showing the waterways of Süleymaniye Complex, this building is indicated as the classroom. In an old photo, the darülkurra has lost its roof and is surrounded by buildings. During the restoration carried out by A.S.Ülgen in 1950's, the accretions around it were removed and its dome was reconstructed.

Istanbul, Süleymaniye, timber houses

The primary school is located to the east of the Evvel Medrese, above the eastern end of the Tiryaki Bazaar. From a small door on Süleymaniye Street, one enters a garden. There is a semi-open space covered by a dome at the entrance. This was used as the summer classroom. The closed part of the school is rectangular in plan. The primary school is used as a library for children today.

The hospital, darüşşifa is a spacious building, located to the southwest of the mosque, on a terrain sloping towards the west. It is organized around two courtyards. A pharmacy and a small bath were attached to it. The foundation deed of the complex lists the qualifications of the doctors who could work in this hospital. To provide health services was not assumed as a public duty in the sixteenth century; so hospitals were established by benevolent people, as part of foundations. Only the sultan and his family could afford such expensive projects. Süleymaniye hospital was the second healthcare center in Istanbul when it was built.

The darüzziyafe, the public kitchen of the complex is to the north of the hospital. It consists of a kitchen, a refectory, storage rooms, a bakery and the administrator's office. The architectural design of the imaret is similar to the public kitchen of the Bayezıt II Complex in Istanbul with its compact organisation and arrangement of the units around a arcaded courtyard. It is a big structure which served the students and the staff of the complex, as well as the guests entertained at the tabhane. Its basement was used as the stable for the animals of the guests staying at the guesthouse.

According to the foundation deed of Süleymaniye Complex, the guests were welcomed at the complex and could stay there for three days, without any charge. During this period, their animals stayed at the stable and were looked after. There are two entrances to the stable; a small one from the sloping street to the south of the building and a large gate from the road along the west wall. The interior is a L shaped large hall, covered with vaults. Slit windows were used for the ventilation and illumination of the interior.

The guesthouse, tabhane is situated to the north of the public kitchen. The monumental gate on Süleymaniye Imaret Street leads to a forecourt from which the building is reached. The guesthouse is a spacious building with rooms and iwans arranged around a courtyard. The courtyard is paved with marble slab and has a pool in the center. The iwan across the entrance is the most conspicuous element of the whole composition. It was reserved for guests, to come together, to have meals or chatting. There are also small sofas in front of the rooms for sitting and resting. The meals were served from the kitchen. In the Republican Period, the guesthouse was assigned to be used as part of the State Archives. It is not open to the public. The earthquake in 1999 caused some damage to its structure. Conservation works are on the way.

Imperial complexes usually have double baths, hamams in their programs. According to the historic documents related to its construction, the bath was one of the last buildings to be completed. Probably due to the constraints in finding a suitable place to build it, the bath of Süleymaniye Complex is a single one, meaning that it can serve men and women at different hours of the day. The planimetry of the hot section has a central dome with four iwans and four corner cells. The bath has undergone some alterations in the nineteenth century. Its three bay porch was walled in to create additional space for the customers. A timber gallery , şırvan was added to the dressing hall. The bath stopped functioning after 1930's, but after a restoration in late 1980's, it is in service again.

Due to the sloping terrain on which the Complex is built, several basements had to be built, which were used as shops or storage areas. Under the terrace on the north side of the mosque, there is a long row of shops. Another long row, attached to the south wall of the third and fourth madrasas, faced these shops. This was a bazaar where craftsmen specialized in brasswork producing samovars, braziers, candlesticks were located. The street is called Dökmeciler, the founders' bazaar. The shops are rectangular in plan and covered by vaults. The timber shutters on their façades have been changed in time. Originally, they had wide eaves which protected the goods exhibited in front of the shops. The evidence for some of the supporting elements are preserved.

Süleymaniye Complex is the greatest of Sinan's projects in Istanbul. It was built at a time when Ottomans were very strong, economically and politically. It reflects the concept of an Ottoman imperial complex, illustrating the building types and the arts and crafts of the sixteenth century. The integrity of the complex has to be preserved with care. The modern uses should be selected carefully, in order to present the site as a socio-cultural institution of its time.

During the sixteenth century, Süleymaniye quarter was a fashionable quarter with houses close to the Old Palace. The popularity of the district continued over the centuries, attracting high ranking officials. The most impressive of the vizierial complexes was the palace of Siyavuş Paşa with 300 rooms, baths, magazines and shops. The panorama by C. Loos, who visited Istanbul in early eighteenth century, gives a good idea about how the area looked before major transformations took place. The urban fabric of Süleymaniye consists mostly of the timber houses from the nineteenth century. The houses usually have two or three floors and roofs covered with traditional tiles. The entrances are raised from the street by a few steps. The upper floors project towards the street or the back garden with jetties.

Süleymaniye is located very close to the harbour area. The coastal strip of this area was reserved to commercial activity since the fifteenth century. Each craft had its workshop on a streets, forming arastas, lines of shops. Commercial activity in the area to the north of Süleymaniye continued within its earlier boundaries until the twentieth century. After 1950's there was a boom; the timber houses in the proximity of the commercial district were pulled down to give way to large scaled reinforced concrete buildings. Several workshops and small industrial plants occupied these multi storeyed structures. Thus Süleymaniye, which was a residential quarter during the Ottoman period, with konaks commanding a nice view over the Golden Horn, lost its attraction. The social structure of the district changed dramatically with many immigrant families from southeast Anatolia. The inhabitants preferred to live there due to its proximity to the commercial center. Almost all the houses were rented or purchased by families with rural background and bachelors looking for job opportunities. During Istanbul's listing to the World Heritage, the timber houses within the district were in better condition than today and reflected the spirit of the place.

2. The ZEYREK quarter

Zeyrek is a traditional neighborhood with significant Byzantine and Ottoman structures . It is located on a hillside overlooking the Golden Horn and Süleymaniye. The quarter is famous for its timber houses surrounding Zeyrek Camii, an important medieval monument, which was originally part of the Pantocrator Monastery founded in the twelfth century by Queen Eirene, wife of John Comnenos II. The construction started in 1118 with the South Church. Then the North Church dedicated to Lady Mary was added. The queen died in 1134 before the complex was finished. Her husband continued the project; she was interred in between the south and the north churches and a chapel was constructed over her tomb.

Zeyrek Camii, eastern elevation

This building, squeezed between two larger structures, was called the Funerary Church.

There is a foundation deed from 1136 which provides information about the program of the monastery and the charity institutions attached to it. According to this important historic document, the monastery comprised a house for the elderly, a hospital and an eye clinic. The complex was occupied by the Venetians during the Latin rule between 1204 and 1261. It was used partially as a storage place for the looted goods from the city, before they were sent to Europe. The monastery and the churches were restored by the Byzantines after they took over the city in 1261.

The dependencies of the monastery have been lost in the course of time. The name Zeyrek comes from the professor who taught at the madrasa established within the Pantocrator Monastery by the Ottomans after establishing power in the city. The madrasa use was temporary. After the completion of the Fatih Complex, the students at Zeyrek moved to the newly constructed madrasas there. The Pantocrator Monastery became Zeyrek Camii and has been used as a mosque since the late fifteenth century.

The monument suffered from several earthquakes during its long history. The style of the repairs provides evidence about the date of interventions. The 1766 earthquake probably resulted in the collapse of the central dome of the north church and produced deformations in the columns of the South Church. As a result of the damages, the columns in both the North and South churches were replaced by piers with larger cross sections. A Sultan's lodge was added to the southwest of the mosque. The damages caused by the 1894 earthquake were followed by repairs which are not documented. During the twentieth century, the responsibility of the monument was assumed by the General Directorate of Pious Foundations. The western and northern façades of the monument were treated by architects working for the General Directorate, A.S.Ülgen and F.Çuhadaroğlu. From the restorations undertaken between 1950-1970, there is not much documentation explaining the decisions for interventions. Following a need for the renovation for the timber floor, Dumbarton Oaks conducted research within the South Church, revealing the beautiful opus sectile decoration in the central part of the naos.

In the second half of the twentieth century, the social profile of the Zeyrek neighborhood changed dramatically. The houses were no longer inhabited by the families who had built or inherited them, but immigrants from southeast Anatolia, coming to Istanbul for jobs preferred to live in this quarter due to the low rents and its proximity to the central business district. The newcomers were not very careful about their environment; they did not have the financial means to take care of the old houses.

Several fires devastated large parts of the Historic Peninsula in the nineteenth and twentieth centuries. The last big fire which destroyed the houses and damaged Zeyrek Mosque started at Çırçır in 1833. Luckily, this part of town was not devastated by the big fires in early twentieth century. So the earlier street pattern of the city was preserved in this part of Fatih. The timber houses dating from the nineteenth and early twentieth centuries reflected the traditional atmosphere of old Istanbul, making it a spectacular site, worthy of designation as a World Heritage site.

Neglect, vandalism, fires and bad repairs to the timber houses of Zeyrek is a great source of concern to conservationists. UNESCO has warned Turkey to take urgent measures to stop demolition of the timber architecture. Some exemplar projects and implementation work has been carried out by Turkish Timber Association and Zeyrek Association, an NGO specifically established to save the heritage assets at Zeyrek, with technical support from UNESCO and ICOMOS Turkey. In order to preserve the authenticity of the building and the site, traditional methods and materials were used in the restoration of house no. 46 on İbadethane Sokak. Timber Association has taken initiative to monitor the area and warn the responsible authorities about the bad interventions and losses. Recently the Municipality of Fatih is restoring some houses with financial support from the Governorate of Istanbul. KUDEB, a control and technical assistance center established by the Metropolitan Municipality of Istanbul is training craftsmen and supervising the works.

3. The zone of the RAMPARTS

With the increase of the city's population in the fourth century, the area contained within the Constantinian Wall became densely populated and was not able to meet the demands for new development. Theodosius II decided to enlarge the city, by extending the boundary of Constantinopolis further to the west. A new wall, called the Theodosian Wall was constructed. The new defense line started at Marmara Sea, where the Marble tower stands today and extended in the northern direction, reaching the Blacherna region. During the fifth century, Blacherna was a suburb with an imperial palace overlooking the Golden Horn. Theodosian Wall stopped roughly at the walls of this Palace. During the medieval

Istanbul, Tekfur Saray

period. Blacherna Palace was enlarged and new walls were constructed to defend the city. The section of the landwall from the medieval period is called the Comnenian Wall due to the reigning dynasty at the time. It starts from the north of the Tekfur Saray and stretches towards the north, reaching the coast of the Golden Horn at Ayvansaray.

The Theodosian Wall was fortified with 99 towers, placed approximately 50 meters apart. The towers of the main wall are usually square in plan. Octagonal towers are placed at points where the wall makes an angle. The towers are given numbers, starting from the Marmara shore. The position of the first tower is very critical. It could defend the attacks from the sea and the shore. So its plan is pentagonal, to provide the chance to shoot from different angles.

The main towers were about 16 m high and had three levels. The ground level was accessible from the land to the east of the wall. Usually the land belonged to people and they used the ground level in peace time. The first floor is at the level of the wall walk. There are windows on the walls of the towers,

Comnenian Wall, Towers B15-B18 and front wall of Leo at Ayvansaray

which made it possible to shoot with arrows. Stairs attached to the eastern side of the main wall lead up to the wall walk.

The third level is the roof of the towers, called the platform level. It is possible to climb to the top of the towers with narrow stairs attached to the eastern side of the tower. The stairs were protected from shooting by the enemy with high curtain walls. The top of the towers were crenellated; from this level, it was possible to shoot at the enemy with arrows and catapults.

The main walls are about 5 meters thick and crenellated. They were built of limestone courses with bands of brick. The exteriors of walls are covered with regular coursed ashlar blocks made of local limestone. After earthquakes, the original construction technique was altered or changed.

In front of the main wall there is the front wall, a lower structure, also fortified with towers. The front wall is 3.85 m thick and reinforced with towers placed at 50 meters. Its towers are rectangular or U shaped in plan. They are smaller in size but important in strengthening the defense line. Being located between the main towers, they make it possible to create additional points of attack in the weaker part of the front line. It was possible to shoot arrows from the windows of the towers and also from the battlements above the wall walk. The construction of the front wall is not as refined as the main wall.

The 16 m wide ditch was another important element of the fortifications. Due to the topography of the area, the ditch could not be horizontal. There are several partition walls in the ditch to hold the water, when it is filled. The sources for water are not known, but assumed that the sources in the western part of the city were used.

The Land Wall represents a good example of ancient Hellenistic fortification. It was very strong and could resist the attacks of different armies more than thousand years. Good design and workmanship helped its walls and towers to resist the ravages of time. Yet several repairs had to be undertaken; some towers had to be reconstructed due to earthquakes.

The entrance to the city was provided by seven gates, located at points which were linked with the street pattern and the topography of the city. Porta Aurea/The Golden Gate was the most important one, used by victorious emperors as they entered the city. The entrance was flanked by two beautiful towers made of marble blocks. The second gate, located to the north of the Golden Gate, is the Belgrad Gate. The ancient names of some gates are not known. They are named according to the direction they are heading for or people who lived around it. The name Belgrade was given to the gate because people who came from Belgrade settled around it in the Ottoman period. The other gates towards the north are named Silivri, Mevlevihane, Topkapı/Cannon, Pempton/Sulukule and Edirnekapı. There were also several secondary gates, mainly used by the military. The first on is situated next to Tower 1, near the Marmara Sea.

The medieval part of the Land Wall, the Comnenian Wall, was built over a sloping terrain. The topography made it easier to defend the city. So the new wall was not designed with three components as the Theodosian Wall; it consists of only one line of defence, supported by high towers. The only gate on this part of the land walls is Porta Caligaria, Eğri Kapı, which is still in use. In the area close to the Golden Horn coast, the land is flat. Making it easy to attack the city. To keep the enemy far from the main wall, a front line called Pempton was constructed. There were several repairs to this part of the wall due to the attacks by foreign troops.

The Land Wall has been subjected to quite a number of tremors after its erection. The construction technique used in the repairs after the 440 earthquake was very similar in detail to the original building, therefore hard to differentiate from the original. The repairs after the 740 earthquake, however are different; some are marked with inscriptions and thus easy to date. Some towers were reconstructed after the earthquakes in the nineth and eleventh centuries. The famous earthquakes of 1509, 1766 and 1894 also caused damages to the Theodosian wall.

The military sifnificance of the Land Wall diminished during the Ottoman period, because the city was no longer situated at the frontier. Yet the Venetian fleet occasionally approached towards the Dardanelles and some precautions were taken at the capital. During the first half of the seventeenth century, grand vizier Bayram Paşa carried out some repairs to the land and sea walls in order to prepare the city for the attack of the approaching Venetians.

By the middle of the nineteenth century, the ruined walls and towers of the Theodosian fortification had become a picturesque ruin. Many travellers and artists walked along the exterior of the town, watching the wild vegetation growing from the crevices of the towers. The city was still confined within the walls and the exterior was reserved to the fields and cemeteries. The engravings and sketches of the ninetenth century artists give an idea about the tranquillity of the area.

Towards the end of the nineteenth century, important changes took place in the vicinity of the southern end of the walls. The leather industry which was located at Kazlıçeşme since the fifteenth century expanded towards the east. New workshops and several other factories were constructed next to the southern end of the Land Wall. The construction of the railroad connecting Europe to Istanbul was another important event. The trains entered the city through a passage which was cut between the towers 6 and 8. The changes related to urbanization and modern development continued during the twentieth century. In 1950s, the construction of the motorway along the coast changed the relationship of the walls with the sea. A new cut was made through the curtain wall between the Marble Tower and the first tower of the Theodosian Wall. The sea was filled to build the road, changing the relationship of the sea and the afore mentioned towers.

The Metropolitan Municipality of Istanbul is responsible for the care of the Land and Sea Walls. During the preparation of the urban plan in 1937, it was decided to form a 500 meter band of protection for the Land Wall. Yet several private buildings existed next to the walls and over the ditch. No systematic work was carried out to remove the structures which had croached in the area. After the listing of the Historic Areas of Istanbul as World Heritage, the Metropolitan Municipality took action to clear the area adjoining the Wall from accretions. This required legal operations, so several cases were sued to expropriate the land and remove the modern buildings next to the Land Wall.

The transfer of the Kazlıçeşme industrial area was another component of the rehabilitation project concerning the environs of the Land Wall. The Metropolitan Municipality of Istanbul engaged expert teams to make a survey of the cultural heritage within the protection belt of the Land Wall. A project was developed for the landscaping of

Theodosian Wall, Towers T5-T6 at Yedikule

the green areas along the Land Wall. Inventory cards were prepared for cultural assets which had not been registered and presented to the Protection Board for registration. Experts had discussions about the preparation of conservation projects for the towers and wall sections.

The Castle of Seven Towers

The Castle of Seven Towers is located close to the southern end of the Theodosian Wall, next to the Porta Aurea, Golden Gate. It was built by the order of Mehmed II, as a castle where the state treasury was kept. It is nearly pentagonal in plan. The four towers on its western side belong to the Theodosian Wall. The three in the eastern part are cylindrical in plan. The entrance to the castle is from the northeast, through an arched gateway. The walls are about 12 meters high. A small settlement developed within the castle during its use through the centuries. On a drawing from the seventeenth century, there is a small mosque and several houses; the towers are covered by conical roofs. After the sixteenth century, one of the eastern towers was used as a prison where occasionally foreign envoys were put in custody. Inside the tower, which

Panorama of Istanbul at the beginning of the nineteenth century by A.I. Melling

is also called the "ambassadors' tower". Inside, it is possible to see the names of some of the imprisoned from the graffiti on the walls.

Yedikule Castle became a museum in 1895. There was a fire in 1905 which devastated the settlement inside the castle. The houses disappeared; today only the lower part of the minaret survives from the mosque. Action was taken by the general directorate responsible for Antiquities in the second half of the twentieth century. Architect Cahide Tamer was responsible for the works carried out between the years 1958-1970. A small open air theater was created at the southwest corner of the garden in order to use the castle for performances during the summer nights. Recently, the Ministry of Culture has leased the Castle grounds to a private firm, which arranges several pop concerts and other performances inside the Castle.

During Istanbul's inscription to the World Heritage List, the commercial part of town, Eyüp, Galata, Bosphorus villages, Scutari and the Prince's island were not included in the file because the registration of these areas as historic urban sites was not accomplished at the time.

The historic bazaar of Istanbul consists of the Grand Bazaar and many caravansarays, built between the fifteenth and the twentieth century. Though the area constitutes an important part of the historic city, due to the hardships of working at the site, it was designated as a historic site at a later date. Earthquakes and lack of maintenance has caused damages to the caravansarays, but with its historic and architectural importance, the commercial center of the city deserves to be annexed to the World Heritage sites of Istanbul.

The designation of Galata and Beyoğlu historic districts as conservation areas was accomplished much later, in 1995.

Galata has a dense urban fabric with monuments going back to medieval period. Necessary steps need to be taken to integrate the basic elements of the old city, like Galata, Eyüp and Üsküdar to the "Historic Areas of Istanbul".

There is common concern among the citizens of Istanbul and Turkey about the future of the city. The protection of the natural assets and cultural properties demands a lot of work and care. To construct new skyscrapers, bridges, roads, underwater tunnels without taking care of their impact on the historic city presents great risks for the historic city. Istanbul has to be protected from pressures and vandalism by the efforts of people who know and appreciate its values. Teams of professionals and volunteers work hard towards this goal. We hope that Istanbul will continue to preserve its outstanding universal value with the support of its citizens and professionals who look for better means of presenting its cultural layers, enabling all the world to appreciate and enjoy it.

GREAT MOSQUE AND HOSPITAL OF DIVRIGI

Divriği is a small town in eastern Anatolia, about 100 km to the southeast of Sivas. The area was inhabited since prehistoric times; the name Tephrice, used by the Byzantines can be traced back to the Hittites. The Seljuks established their hegemony in the area towards the end of the eleventh century. As a vassal state attached to the Seljuks, Mengucek dynasty reigned for a short period around Divriği and Erzincan. At Divriği, Menguceks had a well protected citadel, perched on a steep hill. Due to several wars and ravages of time, only Kale Camii, the mosque erected by Şehin Shah bin Süleyman in 1181 survives from the settlement inside the walls. The town was on the road linking Sivas to Malatya and further south to Aleppo; the ruins of several caravansarays can be seen in the vicinity. In addition to agricultural and commercial activity, the iron ore sources near the town must have supported its economy.

During the 13th century, Mengücek ruler Ahmet Shah and his wife Turan Melike Sultan founded a complex comprising a mosque, a hospital and a tomb in Divriği. The complex was constructed in 626 H/1228/9, outside of the city walls, on the hill overlooking the lower city. A retaining wall and a terrace was built to the southwest of the compound, to facilitate the approach to the site. In old photos from early twentieth century, the hillside around the complex is free of buildings, but the situation has changed over the recent years.

The combination of a madrasa, a mosque and the tomb of the founder was a common theme in medieval Turkish architecture. Most of the religious and educational buildings have the tombs of their founders close to them, so that the benevolent person is remembered and his/her soul is blessed by prayers. In medieval Anatolia, the number of hospitals were scarce and the composition incorporting a mosque and a hospital did not exist before. So, the compound of Ahmet Shah and his wife Turan Melike Sultan was a innovative foundation. The composite structure is a long rectangular building measuring 32x64 meters; from outside, the two buildings look like one solid structure. The exterior is adorned with elaborate portals, which protrude from the main structure and attract the attention with their size and rich carvings.

Great Mosque

Measuring 30x38 meters in plan, the mosque occupies the larger part of the compound; it lies almost in the north-south direction, with the main entrance facing the citadel. The inscription over the north portal gives the name of the founder and the Seljuk sultan Alauddin Keykubad bin Keyhusrev, to whom Ahmet Shah was attached. The 14 meters tall north portal rises high above the walls of the mosque and is very monumental with its rich decoration. Since the complex was built by cutting into the hillside, the visible part of the eastern wall is quite low. The muqarnas portal which provides access to the imperial lodge located at the northeast corner of the mosque is the main feature of the eastern façade. The third portal of the mosque is in the middle of the western wall.

The mosque interior is divided into five aisles by four rows of columns. The nave is wider than the side aisles. There are five bays. The second bay of the nave is vaulted with heavy ribs forming a four pointed star. Over the third bay there is a dome with a lantern, which provides light to the interior. The number of windows are quite restricted; the four windows in the lower part of the western wall are regarded as part of a later intervention.

The mihrab is situated in a symmetrical position on the qibla wall. At its center, there is a richly decorated niche with a pointed arch, surrounded by a rectangular frame. Except some special sculptural elements attached or carved into the frame, the moldings surrounding the mihrab are not adorned. Two large torchlike abstract figures are attached to

Divriği, general view of the Great Mosque and the Hospital

the sides. The bay in front of the mihrab is accentuated by a dome which has twelve ribs stemming from an elaborate drum with colonnettes. The four small windows in the drum of the dome provide additional light to the interior. The roof above this dome is in the form of a steep and folded pyramidal cap, which highlights the position of the mihrab.

In the thirteenth century, Anatolian Seljuk architecture had a strong tradition in stone building, which is reflected in the mosques, madrasas and caravansarays from the period. As a result, a sophisticated technique was used in the construction of significant buildings. The interior is covered by vaults which are supported by slender piers. Due to structural problems, some of them have been enveloped with additional masonry which hides their beautiful proportions. A rich variety and ingenuity is exhibited in the design and execution of the vaults. Cross and star shaped vaults have opulent ribs; their center pieces are rich with detail, sometimes very complex. The use of two coloured stone and also paint for decoration of the upper structure adds to the high quality of the original design of the mosque.

The mosque has a minaret attached to its northwest corner. Its square base was enveloped in thick masonry, in order to stabilize the shaft which is out of plumb. According to the inscription over the base, this intervention took place in 930H/1523, under the reign of Süleyman the Magnificient. This is evidence that the mosque had structural problems as early as the sixteenth century, probably due to subsidence of the soil filling the terrace on the west side. There were also earthquakes which aggravated the structural problems and caused damages. Since Divriği is close to the North Anatolian Fault, earthquake impacts are unavoidable. The fact that the decorated vaults are replaced by brick domes is an indication of the extent of the damage to the western part of the mosque in the sixteenth century.

Divriği has a harsh climate, with lots of snow in winter. Originally, the roof of the mosque was flat, as is the tradition in this region. Seasons of neglect caused damages to the upper structure; drastic measures were taken to stop the degradation of the stone structure. The roof of the compound is now covered with metal sheets, to protect the structure from further infiltration of water.

The gates of the mosque are exceptional in their design and execution. The monument incorporates different traditions of decoration. Influences from Central Asia, Iran, Armenia and Egypt are noted by the architectural historians who have studied this extraordinary monument. The wide range of

Divriği, Great Mosque, detail from the north gate

decoration suggests that the masons, craftsmen came from different places and were orchestrated by the architect to compose this extraordinary monument.

The north portal is very monumental and unique in its design. A symbolic tree of life with lots of foliage, palmettes, sun discs, lotus flowers was carved on the north portal. The decoration is not in low relief, as is common in other monuments of the period, but three dimensional, with figures detached from the surface and sometimes rotated to give the portal additional dynamism. The conception of such a sculpture may be interpreted as an outburst of artistic genius.

The west portal is named the "textile portal" due to the patterns of its low relief decoration. According to Professor D. Kuban, this gate is not from the thirteenth century; the western wall was damaged and reconstructed. Kuban claims that only some parts of the portal like the double headed eagle and the hawk are from the original design. Double headed eagle was the badge of the Seljuk sultans and here the figure

Divriği, Great Mosque, detail from the north gate

represents Alauddin Keykubad I, who was the suzerain of Ahmet Shah. The falcon, which is depicted with a bent head, is claimed to represent Ahmet Shah.

The name of the ingenius architect/master builder of the complex is recorded in two inscriptions, one inside the mosque and the other inside the hospital. He was Hurrem Shah, son of Mughith from Ahlat, a town on the west coast of Lake Van and well known for its stone monuments and masons.

A wooden minbar made of walnut tree has come down from the thirteenth century in quite good condition. It has inscriptions giving the date 638 H/1240 and the name of the craftsman, who was Ahmet, son of Ibrahim, from Tibilisi. The timber structure of the maqsura, the private worshiping loggia of Ahmet Shah, is not in very good condition but its fence panels have been preserved. The decoration on the fence panels show similarity to the patterns used in the north portal and have very high quality carving. The pieces do not have any inscription but their style confirms that they belong to the original conception.

The Hospital

The hospital is attached to the southeast wall of the mosque. Though smaller in size (24x32 meters) than the mosque, the western façade of the hospital rises a little higher with its two storey inner arrangement. The monumental entrance on the west wall is a masterpiece with its finely carved arch and intricate decoration. The portal is decorated with palmettes, crescents, stars and discs. With its mullion like column, the rectangular window above the entrance is a unique feature in Anatolian Turkish architecture and adds to the surprises the gate offers to its spectators.

The interior of the hospital is similar to an enclosed madrasa, with a pool in the center and an oculus above. In the lower level, three iwans and several rooms are arranged around an inner courtyard.

Although the plan seems symmetrical, the spatial organization of the interior is not; there is the upper level on the south side. Side iwans are not of the same height; the north iwan rises higher. The central part of the building is separated from the sides by arcades. A pair of cylindrical columns which have interesting patterns on them, support the vaulting on the south side. On the north side, the upper structure is supported by octagonal piers.

The upper level is only partial, with rooms on the south and western sides. A steep staircase attached to the entrance wall leads to the first floor. Another small stairway was used to reach the roof, which was flat in the original design.

The hospital is covered by stone vaults. The vestibule of the hospital is covered by a cross vault with a meticulously

Divriği, Great Mosque, double headed eagle from the west gate

decorated octagonal center. Each of the three iwans on the ground level have a different vault composition. The main iwan is the most richly decorated. The upper parts of the walls are decorated with a fan like relief. The central piece of the star vault has a spiral motif fit into a circle. The ribs have elaborate endings. The main iwan is also interesting with the symbols of the horoscope. The iconography is related to the symbolism of hospitals from the medieval period.

Although historic documents provide information about the types of medicines, their preparation, the types of treatment for the sick and the operations conducted by the surgeons in medieval hospitals of Anatolia, how this hospital functioned

Divriği, detail from the entrance to the Hospital

is not clear. The foundation deed which would describe the duties of the doctors and the staff has not been found. The building might have been used like a clinic, only for day patients. The assistants and caretakers could have used the rooms at the upper level.

The Mausoleum

Ahmet Shah and his family are buried in the big room to the north of the main iwan of the hospital. The tomb is located between the mosque and the hospital; the access is from the hospital but there are also windows establishing visual connection with the mosque interior. There are sixteen graves inside the funerary chamber. Although there are no incriptions on the sarcophagi, the decorated ones are identified as the tombs of Ahmed Shah, his mother Fatma Hatun, his wife Turan Melike and his son Süleyman Shah. Three of the sarcophagi are decorated with turquoise colored glazed tiles. The sarcophagus of Ahmed Shah is the most elaborately decorated of all, with gold medallions and "Ya Allah" written on the glazed tiles. One of the sarcophagi is decorated with gypsum.

The interior is lit by small windows on the east wall and the drum. A high dome on squinches covers the burial chamber. The outer form of the roof is pyramidal; it rests on an octagonal drum and rises high above the roof, marking the position of the mausoleum.

Great Mosque and Hospital of Divriği was inscribed on the World Heritage List in 1985 on the basis of criteria i and iv.

> i) A unique artistic achievement, this cultural property in itself represents one of Islamic Architecture's most beautiful built spaces.
>
> iv) The Divriği mosque is an outstanding example of Seldjukian mosques in Anatolia having neither a courtyard, colonnades nor an uncovered ablutions basin but which (owing perhaps to the harshness of the climate) organizes all religious functions

in an enclosed area. A charitable foundation, the contiguous
hospital makes an already exceptional ensemble even more
interesting thanks to a princely command.

SAFRANBOLU

Safranbolu is a small town, located in northwest Turkey, about 200 km to the north of Ankara. The first signs of settlement in the region go back to the Palaeolithic Era. The ancient name of the region was Paphlagonia; several tumuli and rock cut tombs exist in the surroundings of the town. During the Byzantine period there was a fortified settlement at the spot. The region became part of the Danishmend Principality in the beginning of the twelfth century and changed hands between the Byzantines and Seljuks until the early years of the next century. The first Turkish settlement was probably on the castle hill; the town developed on the southern slopes, towards the east and south. Monuments from the fourteenth century, like the Süleyman Pasha mosque, medrese and bath belong to the Candaroğulları dynasty.

The name Safranbolu comes from saffron and is related to the production of the plant which was used for medicines and cooking, especially the coloring of sweets and rice. The town flourished under the Ottomans; seventeenth century was an important time in its history. Hüseyin Efendi, known as Cinci Hoca because of his influence on Sultan Ibrahim, came from this town. He was assigned high positions in Ottoman administration between 1642 and 1648. The monumental caravansaray he founded in his hometown Safranbolu is a magnificent two storey masonry structure with stables for the animals and rooms for the tradesmen and their goods. The commercial center of Safranbolu grew around Cinci Han; markets for cattle, grains, vegetables and wood were organized in its vicinity.

Another important group of buildings from the seventeenth century is the complex of the grand vizier Köprülü Mehmet Pasha, who had been in exile in Safranbolu for some time.

The single domed mosque, which is dated to 1662, is still in function but the madrasa has been lost in time. The nearby arasta of shoemakers, with its shops and a coffehouse belonged to the foundation of Mehmet Pasha as well. Izzet Mehmet Pasha (1743-1812), the grand vizier to Sultan Selim III, is another high level statesman who originated from Safranbolu. He contributed to the embellishment of the town by founding a complex comprising a beautiful mosque and a library in Baroque style. Public libraries were quite rare in Anatolia during the eighteenth century, so the donation of the grand vizier is a valuable contribution to his town.

The main economic activities of Safranbolu were agriculture and commerce. It was a stopping point on the trade route from Sinope, on the Black Sea, to Gerede and other cities of central Anatolia. There were several guilds working on copper, leather and crafts related to agriculture and animal husbandry. The bazaar area of Safranbolu has streets lined with shops belonging to coppersmiths, blacksmiths, tinners, saddlers and makers of pack saddles. Production of traditional sweets made of sesame seeds, Turkish delights and other delicacies was very developed in Safranbolu. Some of the

Safranbolu, houses

traditional crafts are still active, with an effort to overcome the difficulties arising from the changes in the life style.

The old tannery of Safranbolu was located near the Tabakhane stream; thus had easy access to water which was essential for tanning. Due to the modernization of the tanning technology in the ninetenth century, the export of hide dwindled and the tanneries in Safranbolu had to close by mid-twentieth century. The deserted tannery of Safranbolu, which has an interesting timber structure and preserves all its inner fixtures, is an exceptional piece of industrial archaeology from the nineteenth century.

The topography of the town is exciting with deep canyons cut into a high plateau. The central part of Safranbolu developed around Akçasu and Gümüş

Safranbolu, a timber frame house with shops on the street façade

brooks. These small streams run in deep valleys cut into the hills which protect the town from strong winter winds. Gümüş flows down from the north and meets Akçasu brook in the center of town; they converge and become Tabakhane stream.

The city has an organic relationship with water; there are about fifteen small bridges joining the two sides of the brooks. The builders of Safranbolu did not hesitate to build over the water; the love of nature and the close relationship with water is also exhibited in the houses of Safranbolu. The small mosque of Kaçak/Lütfiye with its elegant timber minaret is built over a bridge on Akçasu brook. The mosque is connected with a primary school and a coffee house which gives the local people the chance to enjoy being close to water and listen to its musical sound.

The commercial and residential part of town located at the bottom of the Akçasu valley was called Çukur, meaning the pit. The houses of Safranbolu are arranged over the hills in such a way that they have nice views. In urban areas, streets are narrow and winding, suited to the topography. There are dead end streets, which is typical for many Turkish towns. In the center of town, commercial activity continues along the streets; some houses have shops on their ground floors.

The streets are paved with cobblestones. The roads are inclined towards the middle line, in order to collect the rainwater and drain it down the slope. To protect the private domain of the family from the gazes of the passers-by, the garden walls are high. The household and the guests enter through the house door or gates on the garden wall. Donkeys or horses helped the people to carry things around. The corners of the garden walls were chamfered to ease the movement of the animals on the streets .

Safranbolu is surrounded with woods which supply good quality timber for building. The houses have good solid timber frames, which can resist earthquakes. Houses are nearly square in plan and have tiles on their roofs. The ground floors have masonry walls but are open to the garden. An interesting aspect of the ground floor elevations is the presence of big apertures placed above the gates or next to the entrances. These are windows without glazing. In order to separate the house from the street, the openings were screened by gilistes, laths arranged vertically or at angles. This thick trellis work was good for privacy and also allowed the movement of air; a lot of light came in through the latticework. Sometimes as high as the ground floor or the first floor, these openings add an attractive texture to the house façades.

Due to the relationship with agricultural activity, many families had pack animals and carts and the spaces to accommodate them either were either on the ground level or in the garden. Gardens were used for flower or vegetable growing and for recreation. Many had kameriyes, bowers which were used for entertaining guests and spending time in the open space. Some of the houses have fountains or pools on their first floors. People sit around the pool and chat, enjoying the sound of the water. This is a luxury, exhibiting a high level of living culture.

The upper floors are cantilevered, offering a good view over the garden or the street. The houses on winding streets have triangular projections to correct the geometry of the first floor. The system of the jetty is richly variegated, offering interesting combinations. Bay windows are also a common element of the houses. The ceilings are beautifully decorated with elaborate medallions, timber carvings and patterns made with laths.

Some of the houses are plastered and white washed. So they are white except the corner posts, window frames and shutters. Many of the houses are not plastered. Their closely spaced studding and braces are exposed. The color of the timber is reddish brown, the infill with clay or brick has a creamy color. The alternation of the two materials gives a striped look to the Safranbolu house. The padlocks and latches on the doors reflect the fine art of the local blacksmiths. In general the exteriors of the houses have little decoration, except some dates or Masallah medallions which are placed under the eaves.

Since there is not much ventilation of air at the bottom of the valley, during the hot season people of Safranbolu took refuge in the spacious gardens to the west of the city. Many of the well to do families had houses in the center and also a summer mansion at Bağlar, where the settlement pattern constitutes of houses within orchards; the natural setting is impressive and beautiful. The vineyards and fruit trees in the gardens of the summer houses gave the households to prepare syrups and dried fruits for the winter.

During the Ottoman period, the population of the town was multi-ethnic. Kıranköy, the high part of the town, to the west of the center, was the Greek quarter. There was the Church of Hagios Stephanos (now Ulu Cami), several schools, shops and houses. Greeks were merchants, craftsmen, builders. Their houses were similar in structure and form to the ones in the center. Some had wine cellars. As a result of the exchange of population between Greece and Turkey in 1923, the Greek quarter was deserted.

Until the middle of the twentieth century, Safranbolu had a self sufficient economy depending on agriculture and trade. The people of Safranbolu were closely related to farming and the fields. Safranbolu was not affected by migration from rural areas and development pressures which damaged or destroyed many of the historic centers in Turkey. In the early years of the Turkish Republic, Karabük, which is 7 km from Safranbolu was chosen as the location to establish the first Iron and Steel Factory of the country. The decision was made in 1937 and the plant started production in 1939. Possibility for jobs attracted many people from the villages to this newly established center, so Safranbolu was spared the pressure of uncontrolled urban sprawl and could preserve its integrity.

Yet as the years passed, Karabük expanded tremendously; Safranbolu lost its significance as a center; its role was diminished to a dormitory town. The houses in town started to change hands; people coming from the villages bought some of the old houses and felt free to make repairs and changes. This was a critical moment because the well preserved town was falling into disrepair and lack of funds and technical assistance could result in its loss.

In early 1970's, there was an attempt to preserve the city. The mayor of Safranbolu K. Ulukavak was interested in taking action to save his town. He cooperated with the Istanbul Technical University, Institute for Architectural History and Restoration of the Faculty of Architecture to lead a campaign to put the whole town under legal protection and develop a conservation plan. In 1975, a symposium was organized in Safranbolu, within the framework of the European Architectural Heritage Year, to raise awareness and make Safranbolu's value known by its people, artists, scholars and the authorities responsible for conservation of cultural heritage. Safranbolu Architectural Assets and Folklore Week, which took place at the end of August 1975, was the starting point of a determined movement towards the conservation of the town.

Several surveys and restoration projects were developed as academic contributions to the documentation of the urban fabric and its conservation. The elaboration of planning decisions for the protection of the town and its monuments was a priority and it was achieved. A total of 1131 historic buildings were scheduled as worthy of protection. 800 Safranbolu houses were registered. Besides the houses, there are more than a hundred fountains, about thirty mosques, fifteen bridges, numerous commercial buildings and several baths that make up the urban fabric. In order to preserve this rich heritage there has to be regular maintenance. It was essential to revive the traditional skills. Old craftsmen, carperters were invited to cooperate. The Emirhocazade

Ahmet Bey House in Bağlar, which was in a dilapidated state, was saved. A vocational school was established in town, to train technical staff to work in the restoration of cultural heritage.

The possibilities for tourism development were investigated. Touring and Automobile Club of Turkey bought Asmazlar Konak, a historic timber house and restored it. The conversion of a Safranbolu house into a small hotel was to set a good example to the local people for investment in tourism. Kaymakamlar House was restored by the Ministry of Culture and Tourism and turned into a local museum. Dr. R. Günay published his comprehensive study of the Safranbolu houses in 1981, providing information about the history and evolution of the city, the building materials, plan typologies and decorative features of the houses.

In Safranbolu there is great harmony between nature and the city. It has a rich repertoire of civil, religious and commercial buildings, illustrating a traditional town from the Ottoman period. The use of timber in construction and decoration gives Safranbolu a special character.

In 1994, Safranbolu's center and Bağlar area were inscribed on the World Heritage List as number 614 on the basis of criteria ii, iv and v.

> *ii) By virtue of its key role in the caravan trade over many centuries, Safranbolu enjoyed great prosperity and as a result it set a standard in public and domestic architecture that exercised a great influence on urban development over a large area of the Ottoman Empire.*

> *iv) The caravan trade was for centuries the main commercial link between the Orient and Europe. As a result, towns of a characteristic type grew up along its route. With the coming of railways in the 19th century, these towns abruptly lost their raison d'etre, and most of them were adapted to other economic bases. Safranbolu was not affected in this way and as a result has preserved its original form and buildings to a remakable extent.*

191

v) The collapse of the caravan trade had a catastrophic effect on Safranbolu. Its proximity to the Karabük Steelworks has given it a new socio-economic role, but it is still vulnerable to external pressures, and so continuous efforts must be made to preserve the traditional townscape.

In the recent years Safranbolu has become a tourist attraction. The dynamics of tourism supports the regeneration of the city. The restoration of the arasta of shoemakers revived the center; it has a lively and attractive atmosphere. The project injected new life into the old bazaar area. The other big projects were the restoration of Cinci Han by the General Directorate of Waqfs and the conversion of the old governor's office building on the Old Castle area into the local museum.

There are several historic towns in Turkey, but Safranbolu is outstanding with its integrity. Safranbolu is remarkable for its urban texture and traditional buildings; the town was preserved because its citizens cared for it and took good care of their houses. But one has to be careful about the changes to the historic houses; renovation demands may clash with the requirement to keep the authenticity of the site. Traffic and parking needs of the local population and the touristic establishments need to be solved. Garden walls and ground floor façades should not be removed or modified for parking or conversion of ground levels to cafes or restaurants. A management plan is urgently needed. Expert supervision and funding should be available to the site, to control and guide the conservation projects in accordance with World Heritage values.

Note on Usage

Modern Turkish uses the latin alphabet, modified to ensure that there is a seperate letter for each main sound. The spelling thus aims at phonetic consistency. For Turkish place names, publications and special terms this book employs modern Turkish spelling. Proper name have been kept in modern Turkish with one exception - İstanbul has been rendered with normal English spelling using I rather than İ unless it is part of a title. Consonants have more or less the same sound as in English, except that:

c *like j in English*

ç *like ch in English*

ğ *the "soft g". Depending on adjoining letters, this is chopped, pronounced like y in English, or treated a lengthening the preceding vowel.*

ı *is a back, close unrounded vowel which does not exist in English, the nearest equivalent being the phantom vowel in the second syllable of rhythm.*

ö *like ö German or eu in French peur*

ş *like sh in English*

ü *like ü in German or u in French*

BIBLIOGRAPHY

Arseven, Celal Esat - Türk Sanatı (Turkish Art), Cem Yay., İstanbul, 1973.

Aslanapa, Oktay - Anadolu'da Türk Çini ve Seramik Sanatı (Turkish Tile and Ceramic Art in Anatolia), Ankara, 1965.

Aslanapa, Oktay - Türk Halı Sanatı (Turkish Carpet Art), İstanbul, 1973.

Aslanapa, Oktay - Selçuklu Halıları (The Seljuk Carpets); İstanbul, 1973.

Aslanapa, Oktay- Türk Sanatı (Turkish Art), Remzi Kitabevi, İstanbul, 1984.

Atalayer, Günay -"Dünden Bugüne Anadolu'da Kumaş Dokuma Sanatı", Türk Kültüründe Sanat ve Mimari ("Art of Textile in Anatolia from Past to Present", Art and Architecture in Turkish Culture), İstanbul, 1993, p.41.

Atasoy, N. & Çağman, F - Turkish Miniatyre Painting, İstanbul, 1974.

Ayyıldız, Uğur- Pure Silk Turkish Carpets, HEREKE and KAYSERİ, İstanbul, 1983.

Baltacıoğlu, İ.Hakkı- Türklerde Yazı Sanatu (Art of Turkish Calligraphy), Ankara, 1958.

Baykal, İsmail- "Hat Sanatı", (Art of Calligraphy) Güzel Sanatlar Mecmuası, 1940, no. 2,pp.33-48.

Binark, İsmat- Eski Kitapçılık Sanatlarımız (Our Old Book Arts), Ankara, 1975

Deniz, Bekir- Türk Dünyasında Halı ve Düz Dokuma Yaygılar (Carpet and Flat Woven Rugs in Turkish World), Atatürk Kültür Merkezi Yay., Ankara, 2000.

Durul, Yusuf- Anadolu Kilimlerinden Örnekler (Samples of Anatolian Rugs), Akbank Yay., İstanbul, 1985.

Erginsoy, Ülker - İslam Maden Sanatının Gelişmesi, Başlangıçtan Anadolu Selçuklularının Sonuna Kadar (Development of Islam Mine Art, From the Beginning to End of Anadolu Seljuks), İstanbul, 1977.

Erginsoy, Ülker- "Türklerin İslam Maden Sanatına Katkıları", İslam Sanatında Türkler ("Contrubitions of Turks to Islamic Metal Art", Turks in Islamic Art), İstanbul, 1976.

Ersoy, Ayla - "Osmanlı Saray Kilimleri" (Ottoman Palace Rugs) İlgi Dergisi, İstanbul, 1990, no. 61, pp.2-7.

Ersoy, Ayla - XV. Yüzyıl Osmanlı Ağaç İşçiliği (15th Century Ottoman Woodwork), Marmara Üni. Yay., No.509., İstanbul, 1990.

Ersoy, Ayla - "Ebru Sanatı" (Art of Paper Marbling), İlgi Dergisi, İstanbul, 1989, no. 58, pp.24-28.

Ersoy, Ayla- Türk Tezhip Sanatı (Turkish Art of Illumination), Akbank Yay., İstanbul, 1989.

Esin, Emel- "Selçuklu Sanatı Evren Tasvirinin Türk İkonografisinde Menşeleri" (Origins of Seljuk Art's Depiction of Universe in Turkish Iconography), Selçuklu Araştırmaları Dergisi, Sayı I, 1969.

Esin, Emel -Orta Asya'dan Osmanlıya Türk Sanatında İkonografik Motifler (Iconographic Motifs in Turkish Art from Central Asia to Ottomans), Kabalcı Yay., İstanbul, 2003.

Ettınghausen.R.- Studies in Muslim Iconography, The Unicorn, Washington, 1950

Ettınghausen, R. - Turkish Miniature from the 13th to the 18th century, Milano, 1965.

Göktaş, Uğur- "Hatip Ebruları", İlgi Dergisi, İstanbul, 1990, no. 63, pp.32-35.

Grube, E.J.- The Classical Style in Islamic Painting, 1968.

Güngör, Hulusi - Türk Halıları (Turkish Carpets), İstanbul, 1984.

İnal, Günseli- Türk-İslam Minyatür Sanatı Başlangıcından Osmanlılara Kadar (Turkish-Islam Miniature Art from the beginning to Ottomans), Hacettepe Üni. Yay., Ankara, 1976.

İrepoğlu, Gül- "Osmanlı Miniature Sanatında Klasik Dönem" Türk Kültüründe Sanat ve Mimari (Classical Period in Ottoman Miniature Art Art and Architecture in Turkish Culture), İstanbul, 1993, p.73,

Kerametli, Can- "Anadolu Selçuklu Devri Duvar Çinileri", Türkiyemiz (Wall Tiles of Anatolian Seljuk Period, Our Turkey), İstanbul, 1973, no. 10, pp. 2-10.

Kuşoğlu, M. Zeki- "Dünkü Sanatlarımızdan Savat" ("Niello Among Our Arts in the Past), İlgi Dergisi, 1988i no. 55, pp.33-35.

Kuşoğlu, M. Zeki - "Telkari", İlgi Dergisi, 1986, No. 45, pp.31-35.

Kuşoğlu, M. Zeki - "Gümüş Kakma Sanatımız" (Our Art of Silver Inlay), İlgi Dergisi, 1987, no. 48, pp.32-35.

Kuşoğlu, M. Zeki - "Dünkü Sanatlarımızdan Mıhlama" (Nailing Among our Arts in the Past), İlgi Dergisi, 1989, no. 57,pp. 33-35.

Kuşoğlu, M. Zdki- "Unutulmuş Bir Sanat Tombak" (A Forgotten Art, Tombac), İlgi Dergisi, 1986, No. 44 pp. 23-25.

Lane, A. Early Islamic Pottery, London, 1947.

Mahir, Banu- Osmanlı Minyatür Sanatı (Ottoman Miniature Art), Kabalcı Yay., İstanbul, 2005.

Mülayim, Selçuk- Anadolu Türk Mimarisinde Geometrik Süslemeler (Geometrical Ornamentations in Anatolian Turkish Architecture), Ankara, Undated.

Otto-Dorn, K. -Türkische Keramik, Ankara, 1957.

Ögel, Semra-Anadolu Selçukluların Taş Tezyinatı (Stone Embellishment of Anatolian Seljuks), Ankara, 1966.

Ögel- Semra- Anadolu'nun Selçuklu Çehresi (Seljuk Face of Anatolia), Akbank Yay., İstnabul, 1994.

Öney, Gönül - Anadolu'da Selçuklu ve Beylikler Devri Ahşap Teknikleri (Wooden Tchniques of Seljuks and Beyliks in Anatolia), Sanat Tarihi Yıllığı III, İstanbul, 1969-1970.

Öney, Gönül - Ankara'da Türk Devri Dini ve Sosyal Yapıları (Religious and Social Structures of Turkish Period in Ankara), Ankara, 1971.

Öney, Gönül- İslam Mimarisinde Çini (Tiling İn Islamic Architecture), Ada Yay., İzmir, 1987.

Öney, Gönül - Anadolu Selçuklu Mimarisinde Süsleme ve El Sanatları (Embellishment and Handicrafts in Anatolian Sejuk Architecture), Türkiye İş Bankası Kültür Yay., Ankara, 1976, No 185.

Övüç, Refia- Türk İşleme Desenleri (Turkish Embroidery Patterns), Akbank Yay., İstanbul, 1986.

Özçelik, Serpil- "Kilimin Tarihi Geçmişi ve Sembolizm" (History of Rug and Symbolism), Türk Kültür ve Sanatından Kesitler, 21. YY. Vakfı Yay., İstanbul, 2002, p.85.

Özgümüş, Üzlifat- Anadolu Camcılığı (Anatolian Glass Making), Pera Yay., İstanbul, 2000.

Özgümüş, Üzlifat- Cam Eserler Koleksiyonu (Collection of Glass Works), T.Şişe ve Cam Fab. Yay., İstanbul, 1985.

Rıefstahl, R.M.- Primitive Rugs of the Konya Type in the Mosque of Beyşehir, The Art Bulletin XIII.1931, pp.177-220.

Rice, T.-Islamic Painting, A Survey, Edinburgh, 1971.

Thema Larousse, Tematik Ansiklopedi, İstanbul, 1994, Milliyet Yay.

Yetkin, Şerare-Anadolu'da Türk Çini Sanatının Gelişmesi (Development of Turkish Tile Art in Anatolia), İstanbul, 1973.

Yücel, Erdem- "Türk Mimarisinde Ağaç İşleri" ("Wood Works in Turkish Architecture), Arkitekt, İstanbul, 1968, no.329.

Yücel, Erdem- "Selçuklu Ağaç İşçiliği" (Seljuk Wood Work), Sanat Dünyamız, İstanbul, 1975, no. 4.

Yücel, Erdem- "Türk Sanatında Cam İşleri", Türkiyemiz ("Glass Works in Turkish Art", Our Turkey) İstanbul, 1974, no.12, pp.24-25.